Beginning Java™
Google App Engine

Kyle Roche
Jeff Douglas

Apress®

Beginning Java™ Google App Engine

ISBN-13 (pbk): 978-1-4302-2553-9

ISBN-13 (electronic): 978-1-4302-2554-6

9 8 7 6 5 4 3 2 1

President and Publisher: Paul Manning
Lead Editor: Steve Anglin
Developmental Editor: Tom Welsh
Technical Reviewer: Kunal Mittal
Editorial Board: Clay Andres, Steve Anglin, Mark Beckner, Ewan Buckingham, Gary Cornell, Jonathan Gennick, Jonathan Hassell, Michelle Lowman, Matthew Moodie, Duncan Parkes, Jeffrey Pepper, Frank Pohlmann, Douglas Pundick, Ben Renow-Clarke, Dominic Shakeshaft, Matt Wade, Tom Welsh
Coordinating Editor: Kelly Moritz
Copy Editor: Jill Steinberg
Composition: ContentWorks, Inc.
Indexer: BIM Indexing & Proofreading Services
Artist: April Milne
Cover Designer: Anna Ishchenko

Distributed to the book trade worldwide by Springer-Verlag New York, Inc., 233 Spring Street, 6th Floor, New York, NY 10013. Phone 1-800-SPRINGER, fax 201-348-4505, e-mail orders-ny@springer-sbm.com, or visit http://www.springeronline.com.

For information on translations, please e-mail info@apress.com, or visit http://www.apress.com.

Apress and friends of ED books may be purchased in bulk for academic, corporate, or promotional use. eBook versions and licenses are also available for most titles. For more information, reference our Special Bulk Sales–eBook Licensing web page at http://www.apress.com/info/bulksales.

The source code for this book is available to readers at http://www.apress.com. You will need to answer questions pertaining to this book in order to successfully download the code.

There's an Irish saying . . . no man can prosper without his woman's leave. —KR

To Cathy, who has touched not only my heart,
but the hearts of so many that will never remember her. I love you. —JD

Contents at a Glance

Contents

Foreword

You've just picked up a book on Google App Engine. Welcome to the ground floor of a critical component in our industry's shift to cloud computing.

It's not an exaggeration to say that the development of consumer and enterprise applications has been completely transformed by the emergence of cloud computing over the past several years. First came a revolution in application delivery—the idea that applications could be delivered as a service over the Internet, without any software to install or maintain. Then came a revolution in application infrastructure—the idea that developers could consume raw computing and storage capabilities as a service, without any physical infrastructure to deploy or maintain.

Now we're seeing a revolution in application platforms—giving developers the ability to build applications using higher-level building blocks, without needing to know about the underlying physical machine. App Engine is Google's entry into this world of on-demand application development and deployment, and represents a major contribution in this shift to the cloud. Here's why App Engine is so important:

1. Development without worrying about deployment infrastructure

Most application development projects require a lot of time for planning the development and deployment stack. Which app-server container, database server, and load balancer should you use? Do you have enough licenses to deploy? Is your app going to share an existing database or do you need to spin up a new instance? How will you back up and monitor the performance of the app? Do you have enough CPU, data, and network resources to adequately scale your app? All these questions had to be answered before you could write a single line of code. Google App Engine changes all that. Google provides a complete development and deployment stack, and you can start developing with no up-front cost. Google does the heavy lifting, allowing you to focus on the specific needs of your users.

2. Single development environment, end to end

Database development, application development, and UI development have traditionally been done in completely different environments, often by completely different development teams. With App Engine's integration with Google Web Toolkit, you can download the SDK, install the Eclipse plug-in, and start to code your entire application in a single environment. You can build your UI directly in Java, connect it to App Engine Java Data Objects, and debug everything end to end, all from within Eclipse.

3. Instant deployment, cloud scalability

Traditional application developers allocate up to one third of their total development time to deployment into a production environment. Your first App Engine app will deploy from your local development environment to Google's world-class, cloud-scale production infrastructure, all with a press of a button. And your application can scale from its first user to its millionth user with complete elasticity, literally running on the same infrastructure as the highest traffic sites on the Internet.

The implications?

Given Google App Engine's new capabilities, we've been excited to add it to the set of tools that we use at Appirio to help our enterprise customers do more with the cloud. App Engine fills a recognized gulf between the two leading cloud platforms, Force.com and Amazon Web Services. Force.com is a rich business application platform with built-in business objects that allow applications to inherit a broad swath of functionality. But some applications don't require this functionality and would benefit from having greater control and direct access to "lower levels" of the platform. At the other end of the spectrum, Amazon Web Services, in particular S3 and EC2, give application developers the power to control their own infrastructure without the headaches of hardware ownership. But many applications don't require this level of control of the infrastructure; a higher level of abstraction would make development much more efficient.

We see Google App Engine as filling the void between these two leading platforms. App Engine offers more control than you get from working in a Force.com environment. And App Engine offers abstraction over several layers of infrastructure that we'd prefer not to deal with in the applications that we build today on EC2, so, for example, we don't have to worry about the size of the machine we spin up.

The best part is that these technologies are almost completely complementary, and toolkits exist to ease their interoperability. At an event this year, someone posed the following question: "Is the industry on the verge of a new set of platform wars? Or will all the different cloud platforms create an interwoven fabric of web applications that draw from each cloud as is convenient?" We believe firmly in the latter. After all, the real "platform war" is still against the old paradigm. Most developers out there don't know that they don't need to buy hardware and software anymore in order to develop and deploy world-class web applications.

But you will. Enjoy this introduction to the new world of developing on Google's App Engine. We look forward to seeing the applications that you develop!

Ryan Nichols
V.P. Cloud Strategy, Appirio

About the Authors

Kyle Roche has been working in the cloud-computing space since 2005. Professionally, Kyle has over 10 years of experience in the enterprise software space. With deep roots in application architecture and systems management he quickly recognized cloud computing as the future trend and has since led some of the most progressive cloud-development efforts to date for companies like Salesforce.com, Starbucks, and JP Morgan Chase. Kyle is a regular speaker at industry conferences and user-group meetings and is an evangelist for cloud computing. His personal website is http://www.kyleroche.com.

He lives in Denver with his wife Jessica and his three children Aodhan, Avery, and Kelly.

Jeff Douglas is a highly sought-after and award-winning technologist with more than 15 years of leadership experience crafting technology solutions for companies of all sizes. His technology skills were honed during the fast and furious "dot com era," when he provided SAP development services for Fortune 500 companies including Coca-Cola, Anheuser-Busch, Disney Imagineering, Moen, and Ericsson. After years of being a lowly Java developer, in 2006 he ascended into cloud computing. He periodically writes for developer.force.com and actively tries to work the word "chartreuse" into everyday technical conversations. He speaks at industry conferences and enthusiastically blogs about cloud computing at http://blog.jeffdouglas.com.

Jeff resides in Sarasota, FL, with his wife Cathy and four children Scott, Tyler, Brittany, and Kira (adopted). He and his wife have been medical foster parents for over 11 years, caring for more than 75 children.

Kyle and Jeff both work for Appirio, a cloud solution provider that offers both products and professional services to help enterprises accelerate their adoption of the cloud. With over 2,500 customers, Appirio has a proven track record of implementing mission-critical solutions and developing innovative products on cloud platforms such as Salesforce.com, Google Apps, and Amazon Web Services. From offices in the U.S. and Japan, Appirio serves a wide range of companies including Avago, Hamilton Beach, Japan Post Network, Ltd, Pfizer, and Qualcomm. Appirio was founded in 2006, is the fastest growing partner of Salesforce.com and Google, and is backed by Sequoia Capital and GGV Capital.

About the Technical Reviewer

 **Kunal Mittal** serves as an Executive Director of Technology at Sony Pictures Entertainment where he is responsible for the SOA and Identity Management programs. He provides a centralized engineering service to different lines of business and consults on the open-source technologies, content management, collaboration, and mobile strategies.

Kunal is an entrepreneur who helps startups define their technology strategy, product roadmap, and development plans. Having strong relations with several development partners worldwide, he is able to help startups and large companies build appropriate development partnerships. He generally works in an advisor or consulting CTO capacity, and serves actively in the Project Management and Technical Architect functions.

He has authored and edited several books and articles on J2EE, cloud computing, and mobile technologies. He holds a Master's degree in Software Engineering and is an instrument-rated private pilot.

Acknowledgments

This was an exciting title for Jeff and me. It's difficult to get a book together on a technology that was launched just weeks before and releases updates faster then we're drafting chapters. As this was our first printed publication we had a lot to learn about the process. It was a growing experience for us and we want to thank some of the key people who helped make this possible.

First, we'd like to thank our families who gave up a lot of their weekend and evening time to allow this project to get completed. Thanks to my wife, Jessica, and my three children: Aodhan, Avery, and Kelly. And thanks to Jeff's wife, Cathy, who went so far as to proofread all of his chapters before they were sent in, and his children: Scott, Tyler, Brittany, and Kira.

Next, we'd like to acknowledge the team led by Kelly Moritz and Steve Anglin at Apress that coordinated this entire effort. Kelly really helped us through our first printed publication. It's a difficult process and without her guidance this wouldn't have happened. Steve persevered through endless back and forth communications, refining the abstract and the concept for the book. Of course, we'd also like to acknowledge the editing team of Tom Welsh and Matthew Moodie, and our technical reviewer Kunal Mittal, for their patience with two over-eager first-time writers.

Also, thanks to the Appirio team for putting us in a position to write a book on this emerging technology. Appirio is like no other company we've encountered. Having been a part of some of the most progressive cloud-computing projects to date, we constantly get the opportunity to work with cutting-edge offerings, like Google App Engine, as soon as they're available. We'd especially like to thank Ryan Nichols, V.P. of Cloud Strategy for Appirio, who wrote the fantastic Foreword for this book. Ryan is a thought leader in the cloud computing space and we're honored to have him take an interest in our book.

Finally, thanks to all of you for taking that leap of faith from traditional development environments to cloud-based platform development. App Engine is a key component of cloud computing and will no doubt be a platform that runs some of the most exciting web applications we'll see in the next few years. Hopefully, with this foundation, one (or more) of those applications will be yours!

Kyle Roche
Jeff Douglas

Introduction

Application development, as you know it, is about to change. Think about your development project plans for a moment. Do they all seem to have the same line items for the first phase? Build a server. Install a database. Configure the application server. You're a programmer, aren't you? Why spread your talents so thin? You should be able to focus your energy on building the application from day one. That's where Google App Engine comes into the picture. There's no need to ever worry about building a development server, installing a database, setting up an application server, opening ports, and the endless other tasks that come with traditional development. With Google App Engine, you can start building your application right away.

Google App Engine applications are built using the same tools you use today for Java development. The Google Plugin for Eclipse allows you to develop your entire application in a single IDE. Everything from data management to user-interface design is encompassed in the development environment. You no longer need to use a different tool or server for each layer of the application stack. And most importantly, it's an unquestionable advantage to be able to spend less time on setting up the evironment and more time on the application's business value.

We've been there. We used to spend 80% of our time on application maintenance and upgrades and only 20% on innovation. But the industry is evolving. It's time to reverse that formula. Let Google worry about scalability, security, hosting, load balancing, bandwidth, and all the other preparatory and peripheral tasks that accompany writing an application. We invite you to spend your time innovating and concentrate on the business value of your applications, not their foundations.

In this book we're going to take you through configuring your development environment for Google App Engine. You'll build your first application and quickly advance your way through the offerings that come with App Engine. We'll sprinkle some other technologies into the various chapters—such as Spring, Flex, and Google Web Toolkit (GWT).

This book presents some core examples that build on each other, but for the most part, the chapters are isolated enough to enable you to skip around as needed. In the end you'll build a robust application from the ground up, and there are takeaways from each chapter that you can use in your production environment. And if you are looking for code samples, you've picked up the right book. The book is chock-full of detailed examples of all App Engine's services.

■ ■ ■

CHAPTER 1

Beginning Google App Engine for Java

By now, you've heard about cloud computing. It's gone from a forward-looking concept that was adopted quickly by cutting-edge development communities to a serious requirement for a growing number of businesses. This book focuses on Google App Engine, one of the leading cloud-based development platforms on the market. Powering some of Google's own offerings, like Google Wave and Google Moderator, App Engine provides an affordable, efficient, and scalable platform for developing web applications. App Engine supports both a Java runtime, which we'll cover in this book, and a Python runtime.

Cloud Computing and App Engine

A lot of vendors are staking claims to platform offerings "in the cloud." Currently, it's our opinion that Google, Amazon.com, and Salesforce.com are leading the charge in both the development community and the enterprise-computing space. There are three main, accepted levels of cloud-computing offerings. They are Infrastructure as a Service (IaaS),), Platform as a Service (PaaS),), and Software as a Service (Saas).). Each has unique features and benefits, but there are some commonalities as well.

Any cloud-computing offering should have certain characteristics. Above all, it should be multitenant. A key component of a true cloud-computing platform, multitenancy is a type of software architecture where one instance of the offering is used to serve multiple tenants. The alternative, single tenancy, is how you're probably designing solutions today. Each customer (or business group, or client) gets her own server, database, application layer, and interface. In contrast, a multitenant application would have a single instance of all these layers and would partition the client's data programmatically. Multitenancy is a shared trait among offerings at the IaaS, PaaS, and SaaS layers.

At the lowest level, IaaS offers the physical infrastructure (or virtualized physical infrastructure) to tenants with the ability to pay for what they need in terms of computing power. Instead of purchasing servers, software, and physical location, a tenant of an IaaS offering can pay for these components as needed in a more subscription-based fashion. Leading IaaS vendors like Amazon.com offer "pay per CPU hour" pricing for Linux and Windows platforms. The servers are immediately available and you can spin up dozens of servers in a matter of minutes.

At the highest level, SaaS, much like IaaS, offers solutions to the customer on a per-usage model. The major difference is that SaaS offerings completely abstract the physical and application layers from the end user or developer. For example, Salesforce.com (widely consider the best example of a SaaS offering) provides its own customizable user interface and proprietary programming language (Apex) but doesn't expose to the end user the hardware or software layers that power the application. SaaS offerings have an important characteristic when it comes to application upgrades and maintenance: everything is centrally updated. So, when a new feature is released or a patch or upgrade is provided, it's immediately available to all customers.

In between IaaS and SaaS is the PaaS market. PaaS offers a bit more than IaaS, without providing an actual end-user product. PaaS components are typically building blocks or solution stacks that you can use to build your own applications. This is where Google App Engine fits in your cloud-computing portfolio. App Engine is a PaaS offering, currently supporting a Java and a Python runtime to build your scalable web applications without the need for complex underlying hardware and software layers. Google abstracts those layers and lets you concentrate fully on your application. PaaS does have its own set of challenges, however. With PaaS offerings, like App Engine and Force.com, you are restricted by a governor process or application quotas. PaaS governors protect the shared layers of the multitenant platform from being monopolized by one heavy application or runaway code. Application quotas, which Google defines for App Engine applications, define the daily-allotted amount of computing power, space, or bandwidth that any one application is allowed to utilize. With App Engine you have the option to pay for more power or space if needed. See Chapter 2 for more details on the quotas that are defined and their limits.

Consider Figure 1-1 for a moment. Take a look at where the major players sit in relation to the types of cloud offerings we've discussed so far as well as in comparison to each other. You can quickly see that the major offerings seem to build on each other. Amazon Web Services, in the bottom-left section, offers the least customization. It simply removes your need to build out a physical infrastructure, leaving all the management and support to your IT staff. Shifting to the right, you see that App Engine offers just slightly more abstraction, now covering the platform and infrastructure. Let's compare those two scenarios briefly.

Consider a basic J2EE application running on WebSphere. Assume that it meets the requirements for an application that could be run on App Engine. (See Chapter 4 for more information on the restrictions that applications might face on App Engine.) With Amazon's Elastic Computing Cloud (EC2) you can quickly build the Linux stack with a preconfigured Apache server and your choice of Java application server and database. You have to support the operating system, the database, the application server, the security, and all the same components you'd be supporting in an on-premise environment, except the physical machine. This, no doubt, saves time and money. But, IaaS offerings still need provisioning and long-term support at more layers than the application. Now, on the flip side, consider this same application running on App Engine. You don't need hardware provisioned or software installed, and you don't need an application server or a database. All these are wrapped into the core platform offering from Google.

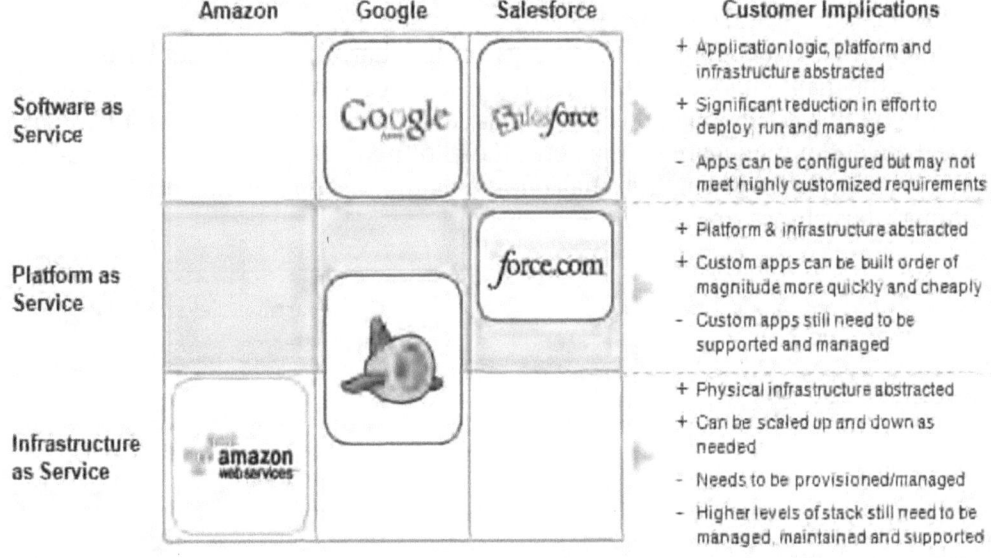

Figure 1-1. *Cloud vendor landscape (Source: Appirio CIO blog)*

Figure 1-1 also shows the Force.com platform in the PaaS sector. It's positioned a bit higher than the App Engine offering, and there's a reason for this. Like some other platform vendors, Force.com encapsulates the runtime environment using its own proprietary language. Apex, the language for Force.com development, looks and feels like Java in many ways but doesn't support the full implementation of any JRE.

It's important to note that the placement of the offerings on this diagram does not indicate preference or correlate with value in any way. Each of these offerings has its own unique value and place in the market. And, in many customer scenarios, we've used a combination of these to build the best solution. In fact, both authors of this book work for a consulting firm (with over 200 people) that has yet to purchase any hardware. We are completely focused on cloud solutions and run our entire business within the three offerings shown in the diagram.

Find More Time to Innovate

Take a look at Figure 1-2, which shows two diagrams comparing the scope of activities and the budget and effort of a traditional IT department with those of another IT department that is leveraging a PaaS offering for its business applications. Take special notice of the amount of maintenance on the hardware, middleware, and application layers for the traditional IT department. It's apparent that all that lost time is intruding on the time, budget, and effort left over for innovation. Now, in comparison, consider the IT department leveraging PaaS offerings for their hardware and middleware layers. Removing the maintenance required to keep those layers in house, the department is free to spend that extra time innovating on its core business applications. You might notice that vendor management is a new time-allotment category when you're using PaaS solutions. However, that's a small effort in comparison to managing these solutions internally.

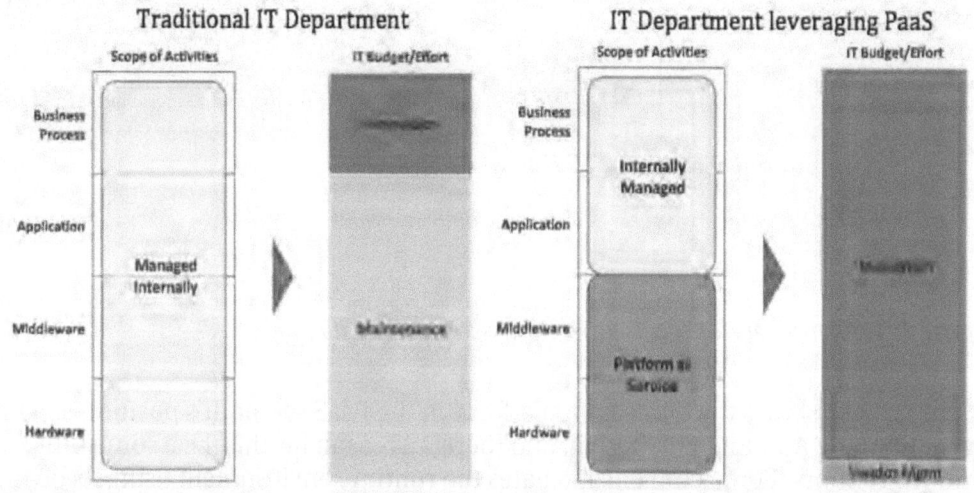

Figure 1-2. *Tradional IT versus IT leveraging PaaS (Source: Appirio CIO blog)*

If you're currently embedded in a traditional software-development structure or a traditional IT department, one of these previous illustrations probably hit home. The inefficiency of traditional IT is one of the main reasons we decided to write this book. The goal was to help you get a jump-start on the major features of Google App Engine for Java, and to give you a platform for building web applications. Let's review some of the skills you're going to learn in the coming chapters.

What You'll Learn in This Book

We've briefly discussed cloud computing and where App Engine fits into the landscape. In Chapter 2 we'll introduce you to more of the underlying architecture for App Engine as well as application quotas. A part of any production application running on App Engine, quotas prevent your application from using too many resources as well as protecting your application from losing resources to other applications.

In Chapter 2, you'll dive right in and sign up for access to App Engine, download the SDK, set up your development IDE, and deploy your first application. If you're going to skip around in the book, make sure you start with Chapter 2, because it lays the foundation and helps you get the tools you'll need to complete the other examples and exercises.

We'll take a step back in Chapters 4 and 5 to tackle a real-world scenario. We'll look at the frameworks and libraries that work well on App Engine and some of the restrictions (and libraries that don't work). Then we'll introduce Google Web Toolkit, and starting from scratch you'll build a timecard application with a rich user interface.

Chapters 6, 7, and 8 cover the service offerings and native tools that come with App Engine. For example, you can leverage Google Authentication services for your applications, which we'll cover in Chapter 6. The App Engine datastore and examples of how to store, query, and index are covered in Chapter 7. In Chapter 8 we'll look at some of the underlying services that the App Engine platform offers your applications. We'll show you how to use App Engine services to send e-mail, send XMPP (Google Talk) messages, manipulate images programmatically, and fetch responses from other web applications.

Finally, we'll cover the Administration Console, the logging functionality, and other maintenance tasks in Chapter 9. We're going to close with a few real-life integration scenarios. First, you'll integrate your App Engine application with Salesforce.com, and then you'll create an App Engine robot for the new and exciting Google Wave offering.

Summary

We have a lot to show you in this book. It's our hope that you'll walk away from it with a solid understanding of the capabilities and features that Google App Engine for Java has to offer. At the time of writing, we covered all the major features of the SDK. If you know Google, you know that they "release early and release often," which makes for a fantastic platform for development as well as a moving target for documentation. Check the online documentation often for updates, and happy coding.

CHAPTER 2

Introduction to App Engine

Google App Engine has been a fantastic disrupter in the technology industry. It's quickly driving innovation among developers and is starting to facilitate a different type of thinking and planning in the enterprise space. App Engine enables you to build enterprise-scalable applications on the same infrastructure that Google uses! The release of Java as the second official language for App Engine marks a tremendous shift in the way applications are being built.

In this chapter we'll cover the basics of App Engine and how it's structured. We'll discuss the major features and benefits of using a platform like App Engine as well as some of the major design considerations (for example, application quotas) that must take place in a multitenant environment.

App Engine Architecture

App Engine is structured differently from the typical web application server. At its core, App Engine restricts your application from any access to the physical infrastructure, preventing you from opening sockets, running background processes (although you can use cron), and using other common back-end routines that application developers take for granted in other environments. Take a look at Figure 2-1. Remember, App Engine is designed to address your concerns about scalability and reliability. It is built on the concept of horizontal scaling, which, in essence, means that instead of running your application on more powerful hardware, you would run your application on more instances of less powerful hardware.

In Figure 2-1 you can see your App Engine application running as an isolated entity within the structure of the multitenant environment. As we discussed in Chapter 1, App Engine shares resources among multiple applications but isolates the data and security between each tenant as well. Your application is able to use some of the Google services, like URL Fetch, to execute processes on its behalf. Because you can't open ports directly within your application, you have to rely on this service, for example, to request Google to open a port and execute the fetch on a URL for the application.

Breaking it down a bit more, consider an apartment building (App Engine) with central air and heating controls. You are a tenant (your App Engine application) in this building. You can't directly adjust the temperature because that would affect the other tenants (other App Engine applications). So, you have to send a request to the building super to change the temperature on your behalf (URLFetch, Bigtable query, Memcache, mail, XMPP, any other Google App Engine service). This is essentially what is happening with App Engine.

If you take a step back, you'll see the long-term implications of this approach. As a developer you now get to ignore scalability concerns like execution time on methods after you have increased data in your datastore. In exchange, you get a fixed duration on execution no matter what your scale becomes. App Engine's response times will be steady from your first request to your millionth request.

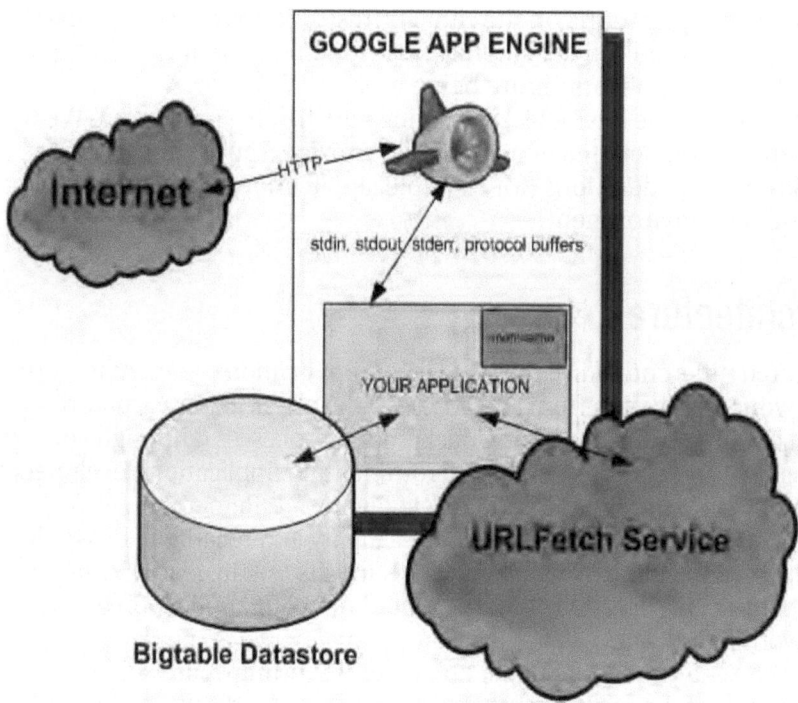

Figure 2-1. *App Engine architecture*

Notice that no file system or components of the architecture represent the physical machine. With App Engine, you have access only to the application layer. There are some open-source projects, for example, Google Virtual File System, that allow you to host an emulated virtual drive on App Engine, but these are not part of the product offering at this time.

Running all these services on behalf of your application isn't something App Engine handles without restrictions. Your application gets a daily limit on each type of request, and each request is recorded and then subtracted from your daily allotment. Let's take a deeper look at these quotas.

Being a Good Neighbor With Quotas

As we mentioned in Chapter 1, App Engine is a multitenant platform. This is far different from hosting your application on a dedicated server or in your own data center. The fundamental difference is that you're not alone! Thousands of other developers are using the same network, hardware, and computing power that Google is offering for use with your applications. At first glance, this might create concern about scalability. Keep in mind that Google is the third largest e-mail provider on the planet and your free App Engine account can scale to five million hits per day. Plus, if you need more than that, you can always pay for more resources.

What if you shared a water source with your next-door neighbor? You wake up on Monday to get ready for work, turn on the shower, and nothing happens. You take a look out the window and notice that your neighbor left the hose on all night after washing his car that afternoon. This shared environment with no restrictions or quotas can be risky. How do you know if you're using too much or if you're neighbor is taking more than his allotment? To protect users from this similar situation with respect to computing power, multitenant platforms use application quotas or governor limits to enforce application restrictions on users. For example, you can have a maximum of 7,400 secure incoming requests per minute on a free App Engine application. With billing enabled (more on that later in this chapter) you can have 30,000 secure incoming requests per minute. The point is, there's a limit on what you can use. This protects other users on the same platform from being affected by applications that have significantly more traffic and resource needs. (This is known as "the slashdot effect." See http://en.wikipedia.org/wiki/slashdotted.)

■ **Note** If you need more resources than the billing-enabled quotas allow you can request an increase by visiting http://code.google.com/support/bin/request.py?contact_type=AppEngineCPURequest.

Billable and Fixed Quotas

App Engine defines two different types of quotas, as shown in Table 2-1.

Table 2-1. *App Engine Quota Types*

Quota Type	Description
Billable Quota	• Maximums are set by the user • Budget-based • Vary by application and can be set by the administrator
Fixed Quota	• Maximums are set by App Engine • System-based • Same for all applications on App Engine

Most applications, and surely everything we show you in this book, will fit well within the fixed quota limits of the free version of App Engine. Enabling billing on your App Engine application increases your quota limits beyond what is provided with the free version. You'll see an increase in the fixed allotment of resources. And, if you still need more, you can define a budget and allocate resources from there. Figure 2-2 shows the App Engine budgeting utility.

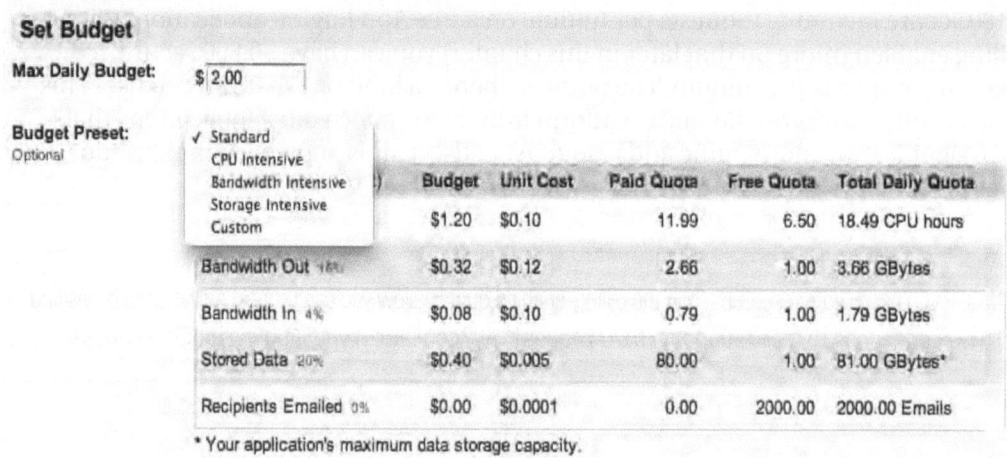

Figure 2-2. *App Engine budget tool*

You may be saying to yourself, "So, I run out…now what?" Quotas roll over each night at midnight. Whatever usage you had starts over with the new calendar day. (App Engine uses Pacific Standard Time for billing and quota measurements, so it may not be midnight in your location.) As you saw in Figure 2-2, you have the option to set daily quota budgets. If your resources exceed what your budget allows, App Engine considers those resources depleted and you'll have to either increase your budget or wait for the next calendar day to get replenished. Except for data storage, which is a rolling metric, all resource measurements are reset at the beginning of each day.

In addition to the daily quotas we've already discussed, App Engine measures a few per-minute quotas. These are subsets of your daily allotment of resources but have unique restrictions for per-minute usage. This is intended to protect your application from using its daily allotment in a short period of time. And, of course, being a multitenant environment, it also prevents other applications on App Engine from monopolizing any one resource and affecting your application's performance. If your application consumes a resource too quickly, the word "Limited" will appear next to the quota line item in the Quota Details screen of your App Engine Administration Console. Once a particular resource has been depleted, App Engine will deny requests for that resource, returning an HTPT 403 Forbidden status code. This may mean that your application will no longer function until the resource has been replenished. The following resources have this type of behavior:

- Requests
- CPU Time
- Incoming bandwidth
- Outgoing bandwidth

For other resources that are depleted, the application will throw an exception of type OverQuotaError. This can be caught and handled and you can respond accordingly. For example, you may want to display a more friendly error message.

■ **Note** The OverQuotaError exception is not yet available for Java applications.

You're probably wondering whether you can query your application usage through the API. Unfortunately, if you're using Java on App Engine, it's not possible (yet). For Python applications on App Engine, you can query your application's CPU usage by calling the Quota API.

Detailed Resource Quotas

The next section will cover in more detail the specific quotas for the various resource types as of version 1.2.5. For up-to-date information, reference the App Engine online documentation, located at http://code.google.com/appengine. Keep in mind that you can purchase additional billable resources through your application's Administration Console.

Requests

App Engine Requests include the total number of requests to the application. If you have billing enabled, there is a per-minute quota for the application, which allows for up to 500 requests per second. That's over a billion per month! Table 2-2 shows the types of resources that are included in the Requests allocation bucket.

Table 2-2. App Engine Quotas for Request Resources

Resource	Daily Limit (Free)	Maximum Rate (Free)	Daily Limit (Billing Enabled)	Maximum Rate (Billing Enabled)
Requests (all requests to application)	1.3M requests	7,400 req / min	43M requests	30,000 req / min
Outgoing Bandwidth (billable includes HTTPS)	1GB	56MB / min	1GB free; 1,046GB max	740MB / min
Incoming Bandwidth (billable includes HTTPS)	1GB	56MB / min	1GB free; 1,046GB max	740MB / min
CPU Time	6.5 CPU-hrs	15 CPU-mins / min	6.5 CPU-hrs free; 1,729 CPU-hrs max	72 CPU-mins / min

Let's take a deeper look at each of these metrics to see how they're calculated.

- *Requests and Secure Requests:* The total number of requests over HTTPS to the application. These requests are measured separately but also count toward the total number of requests.

- *Outgoing Bandwidth (billable):* The amount of data the application sends in response to requests. This includes responses over HTTP, HTTPS, outbound e-mail messages, and data in outgoing requests from the URL Fetch service.

- *Incoming Bandwidth (billable):* The amount of data received by the application from inbound requests. This includes data over HTTP, HTTPS, and responses from the URL Fetch service.

■ **Note** Secure Outgoing Bandwidth and Secure Incoming Bandwidth both carry their own measurements. Both of these metrics count toward the overall measurement as well.

- *CPU Time (billable)*: The measurement of the total processing time the application is using to handle requests. This includes time spent running the application and performing datastore operations but excludes time spent waiting for the responses from other services. For example, if your application is waiting for a response from a URL Fetch request, you are not using CPU time for that transaction.

CPU time is reported in *seconds.* This is equivalent to the number of CPU cycles that can be performed by a 1.2 GHz Intel x86 processor in that amount of time. The actual number of cycles may vary and depends on the conditions internal to App Engine. The number is adjusted for reporting purposes by using the 1.2 GHz processor as a benchmark.

If you're using Python on App Engine you can profile your application in a bit more detail during a transaction. See the online documentation on App Engine for more details. Hopefully, the ability to query your current quota usage statistics will be available for Java applications soon. If you're an administrator of Java applications you can use the Administration Console to examine the logs and see how much CPU time has been used for each request to your application. Here are a few key things to consider when designing your application that may help conserve resources.

- Writes to the datastore use approximately five times the CPU resources as reads from the datastore.

- More resources are needed for datastore writes that require an update to indexes.

- The more properties an entity has defined the more resources App Engine will require to write that entity to the datastore.

- Queries are generally created equal with respect to resource utilization. However, fetching results can require additional CPU time.

Partial Units

App Engine will bill for partial units as they are incurred. Your actual usage of any resource on a given day will be rounded down to the nearest base unit and then rounded up to the nearest cent. The base units are as follows:

1. *CPU Time*: 1 megacycle = 1/1200 CPU second

2. *Bandwidth in/out*: 1 byte

3. *Storage*: 1 byte

4. *E-mail*: 1 e-mail

Datastore

The datastore has its own set of measurements and can be budgeted as well. The metrics and their free and billable quota limits are outlined in Table 2-3.

Table 2-3. *App Engine Quotas for Datastore Resources*

Resource	Daily Limit (Free)	Maximum Rate (Free)	Daily Limit (Billing Enabled)	Maximum Rate (Billing Enabled)
Datastore API Calls	10M calls	57,000 calls / min	140M calls	129,000 calls / min
Stored Data *	1GB	None	1GB free; no max	None
Data Sent to API	12GB	68MB / min	72GB	153MB / min

Resource	Daily Limit (Free)	Maximum Rate (Free)	Daily Limit (Billing Enabled)	Maximum Rate (Billing Enabled)
Data Received from API	115GB	659MB / min	695GB	1,484MB / min
Datastore CPU Time	60 CPU-hrs	20 CPU-mins / min	1,200 CPU-hrs	50 CPU-mins / min

Stored data is a constant metric. It does not replenish at midnight.

The datastore metrics are pretty impressive. It's hard to think of any other application where my maximum data storage was "unlimited." You do pay for space, but the idea that you can't run out of it is pretty fascinating. Here are some descriptions that better describe what the datastore metrics are and how they are measured.

- *Datastore API Calls*: Basically, the total number of CRUD operations on the datastore. Every time your application creates, retrieves, updates, or deletes an entity from the datastore, this metric increases. Queries also count toward your datastore API limits.

- *Stored Data*: As we mentioned above in Table 2-3's footnote, this is not a rolling metric. Data storage is constant and does not replenish day to day, and in the datastore, it's a bit complicated to accurately estimate. There's a certain amount of overhead attached to storing an entity in the datastore. To do this, the following types of metadata are required:

  1. Each entity requires a key. This includes the kind (type), the ID or key name, and the key of the entity's parent entity.

  2. The datastore is schemaless. So, the name and value of each property must be stored in the datastore. This is very different from a relational database where you are storing only the data values. For each entity's attributes you have to store the name and the value in the datastore.

3. You must store built-in and custom index rows that refer to the entity. Each row contains the kind (type) and a collection of property values for the index definition.

- *Data Sent to / Received from the API:* Just like it sounds, App Engine measures how much data is requested from the datastore when retrieving entities or performing queries and how much data is sent to the datastore when creating or updating entities or performing queries.

- *Datastore CPU Time:* This measurement also counts toward your CPU time quota. But with respect to datastore operations, CPU time is measured separately as well. It's calculated and summarized using the same benchmark 1.2GHz CPU.

The datastore has some unique issues related to indexing, which is a more advanced topic. Datastore indexes do count against your application's storage quota. Table 2-4 shows which data is stored for various indexes to help you estimate how much your indexes are consuming.

Table 2-4. *Datastore for Indexes*

Index Type	Rows Used	Data per Row
Kind – querying entities by type	One row per entity	Application ID, kind, primary key, small formatting overhead
Property – querying entities using a single property value	One row per property value per entity. Db.Blog and db.Text value types are excluded. ListProperty properties will return one row per value in the List	Application ID, property name, property value, primary key
Composite – querying entities using multiple property values	One row per unique combination of property values per entity	Application ID, value1, value2,… where value* is a unique combination of values of properties in the composite index

Mail

App Engine for Java utilizes the Mail API to allow your applications to send e-mail messages programmatically. Although the measurements you see in Table 2-5 carry their own metrics, each also contributes to the request-level metrics that encompass these detailed line items. For example, outgoing data over the Mail API will increase your outgoing bandwidth measurements. Table 2-5 shows the specifics for the Mail API quotas.

Table 2-5. App Engine Quotas for Mail API Resources

Resource	Daily Limit (Free)	Maximum Rate (Free)	Daily Limit (Billing Enabled)	Maximum Rate (Billing Enabled)
Mail API Calls	7,000 calls	32 calls / min	1.7M calls	4,900 calls /min
Recipients E-mailed	2,000 recipients	8 recipients / min	2,000 recipients free; 7.4M max	5,100 recipients / min
Admins E-mailed	5,000 mails	24 mails / min	3M mails	9,700 mails / min
Message Body Data Sent	60MB	340KB / min	29GB	84MB / min
Attachments Sent	2,000 attachments	8 attachments / min	2.9M attachments	8,100 attachments / min
Attachment Data Sent	100MB	560 KB / min	100GB	300MB / min

This e-mail allocation is hefty, even for the free account. Let's take a deeper look into each of these measurements to see how App Engine calculates them.

- *Mail API Calls*: The total number of times the application accesses the mail services to send an e-mail message.

- *Recipients E-mailed*: The total number of recipients to whom the application has sent e-mail messages.

- *Admins E-mailed*: The same as the Recipients E-mailed metric but related to application administrators. You get a separate allocation for administrators.

- *Message Body Data Sent*: For each e-mail message that is sent by your application, App Engine measures the amount of data in the body of the e-mail. This metric also counts toward your Outgoing Bandwidth quota.

- *Attachments Sent*: The total number of attachments sent with your e-mail messages.

- *Attachment Data Sent*: For each e-mail message that is sent by your application, App Engine measures the amount of data sent as attachments. This is in addition to the Message Body metric and also counts toward your Outgoing Bandwidth quota.

URL Fetch

App Engine can communicate with other applications or access other resources on the web by fetching URLs. An application can use this service to issue HTTP and HTTPS requests and receive responses. Table 2-6 shows the quota limits for the URL Fetch quota.

Table 2-6. App Engine Quotas for the URL Fetch Service

Resource	Daily Limit (Free)	Maximum Rate (Free)	Daily Limit (Billing Enabled)	Maximum Rate (Billing Enabled)
URL Fetch API Calls	657,000 calls	3,000 calls / min	46M calls	32,000 calls / min
URL Fetch Data Sent	4GB	22MB / min	1,046GB	740MB / min
URL Fetch Data Received	4GB	22MB / min	1,046GB	740MB / min

Here are the descriptions and calculation models for each of these metrics. The URL Fetch service is covered in Chapter 8 in more detail.

- *URL Fetch API Calls*: The total number of times the application accesses the URL Fetch service to perform an HTTP or HTTPS request.

- *URL Fetch Data Sent*: Each request to the URL Fetch service gets measured for data sent as part of the request. This also counts toward your Outgoing Bandwidth quota.

- *URL Fetch Data Received*: The amount of data received in response to a URL Fetch request. This also counts toward your Outgoing Bandwidth quota.

XMPP

XMPP is new as of version 1.2.5 of the Java SDK for App Engine. This service allows your App Engine application to interact with XMPP services like Google Talk. We'll show an example of that type of application in Chapter 9. Table 2-7 shows the limits for the XMPP services.

Table 2-7. *App Engine Quotas for the XMPP Service*

Resource	Daily Limit (Free)	Maximum Rate (Free)	Daily Limit (Billing Enabled)	Maximum Rate (Billing Enabled)
XMPP API Calls	657,000 calls	3,000 calls / min	46M calls	32,000 calls / min
XMPP Data Sent	4GB	22MB / min	1,046GB	740MB / min
XMPP Recipients Messaged	657,000 recipients	n/a	46M recipients	n/a
XMPP Invitations Sent	1,000 invitations	n/a	100,000 invitations	n/a

XMPP is a fantastic new addition to the App Engine API. Google Talk users can chat with the application or send notifications from the application to a Google Talk user who is online. Chapter 9 covers a few of the more advanced topics around App

Engine development, and interacting with a Google Talk user will be one of those examples. Let's take a quick look at how the XMPP quota calculates these metrics.

- *XMPP API Calls*: The total number of times the applications accesses the XMPP service.

- *XMPP Data Sent*: The amount of data sent by the XMPP service. As with the other data metrics, this counts toward your Outgoing Bandwidth quota.

- *XMPP Recipients Messaged*: Each time you communicate with a recipient over the XMPP service, App Engine subtracts from this quota measurement.

- *XMPP Invitations Sent*: To initiate a chat with another party you may need to send invitations. This metric represents the total number of invitations sent by the application.

Image Manipulation

To manipulate image data, you can use App Engine's dedicated Images service, which allows you to resize, rotate, flip, and crop images. You can use the Images service to construct a composite of multiple images and convert images from one format to another. The service also provides a predefined algorithm for photo enhancements. These Images service features count against the following quota. The exact measurements are listed in Table 2-8.

Table 2-8. App Engine Quotas for the Images Service

Resource	Daily Limit (Free)	Maximum Rate (Free)	Daily Limit (Billing Enabled)	Maximum Rate (Billing Enabled)
Image Manipulation API Calls	864,000 calls	4,800 calls / min	45M calls	31,000 calls
Data Sent to API	1GB	5MB / min	560GB	400MB / min
Data Received from API	5GB	28MB / min	427GB	300MB / min
Transformations executed	2.5M transforms	14,000 transforms / min	47M transforms	32,000 transforms / min

Here's some more information on how the Images service calculates the measurements for the quotas described in Table 2-8.

- *Image Manipulation API Calls*: The total number of times the application accesses the Images service.

- *Data Sent to API*: The amount of data sent to the Images service. Because this is internal to App Engine, this metric does not consume Outgoing Bandwidth.

- *Data Received from API*: The amount of data received from the Images service.

- *Transformations executed*: The number of times the service has performed a transformation on an image for the application. Transformations include resizing, rotating, flipping, and cropping images. Other more advanced transformations are included in this metric as well.

Memcache

Sometimes it's more efficient for your application to create an in-memory data cache for persistent storage across some tasks. Memcache serves this purpose for App Engine applications. Table 2-9 outlines the quota measurements for the Memcache service.

Table 2-9. *App Engine Quotas for the Memcache Service*

Resource	Daily Limit (Free)	Maximum Rate (Free)	Daily Limit (Billing Enabled)	Maximum Rate (Billing Enabled)
Memcache API Calls	8.6M	48,000 calls / min	96M	108,000 calls / min
Data Sent to API	10GB	56MB / min	60GB	128MB / min
Data Received from API	50GB	284MB / min	315GB	640MB / min

The Memcache service is covered in Chapter 8, but here are a few more details on how the measurements are calculated.

- *Memcache API Calls*: Total number of times the application accessed the Memcache service to get, set, or expire values.

- *Data Sent to / Received from API*: The total amount of data sent to and from the Memcache service.

Components of an App Engine Application

Building scalable applications with Google App Engine for Java (GAE/J) is similar to building Java applications in your typical on-premise environment with one large exception: there's no need for the network, hardware, operating system, database, or application-server layers of the stack! With Google App Engine for Java, and Platform as a Service offerings in general, you can start to innovate and develop on your application right away and forget about the laborious tasks like setting up the OS and configuring the database. Google App Engine for Java provides a Java 6 JVM and a Java Servlet interface, and supports standard Java technologies like JDO, JPA, JavaMail, and JCache. Google App Engine for Java applications can be developed using the Eclipse IDE, and the Google Plugin for Eclipse even provides a local development server and deployment tools when you're ready to go live with your App Engine application.

There are a few standard components to any Google App Engine for Java application. Some of these are optional if you're using other technologies in their place. For example, the Users service is a great way to provide a trusted authentication mechanism to your user base. But, if you're developing a Facebook application on the App Engine platform, you might be using Facebook Connect from Facebook's native authentication services, in which case the Users service might not be relevant. Table 2-10 gives you a quick look at the basic core components of a standard Google App Engine application.

Table 2-10. Standard App Engine Technology Stack

GAE / J service	Description
JRE	Google App Engine for Java provides a standard Java 6 JVM and supports Java 5 and later. It also uses the Java Servlet standard, which allows you to serve JSP pages and standard files.
Datastore	Google App Engine for Java provides a persistent, scalable, fast datastore built on the DataNucleus Access Platform. You can use JDO and JPA to interact with the datastore and leverage the Memcache API for transient distributed storage for queries results and calculations.

GAE / J service	Description
Schedule Tasks	Google App Engine for Java, via the Administration Console, provides an interface for application owners to create and manage cron jobs on App Engine. More on that in Chapter 9.
Java Tools	The Eclipse IDE, Google Plugin for Eclipse, the local development server, Apache Ant, and Google Web Toolkit (and much more) are available for use on Google App Engine for Java.

Summary

Now that we've covered how App Engine works and we've reviewed the different quotas and their limits, you're ready to start coding. It's important to note that these quotas can change frequently. Reference the online documentation for the current limits and pricing. In the next chapter you'll set up your development environment and get started coding for Google App Engine for Java. You'll start by installing the Google Plugin for Eclipse and creating some small sample projects, and then you'll move on to tackle a more complicated application.

■ ■ ■

Getting Started with Google App Engine for Java

In this chapter we'll walk you through all the components you need to start developing on Google App Engine. The first steps are acquiring the App Engine SDK, setting up the local development environment, and creating your first App Engine project using the local development server.

As we've discussed, App Engine provides a set of major features in addition to the Java 6 JVM. App Engine supports Java servlets, JDO, JPA, JCache, and JavaMail. In traditional software environments you'd have to replicate your production environment by building a development environment to properly test your applications. App Engine provides a lightweight, local development server that allows for quick testing and debugging of all features. This even includes a development authentication engine.

Where Do We Start?

Like any other platform or development environment, the first step is to download and configure the SDK and the development environment. Google App Engine for Java uses the Google Plugin for Eclipse to enable your Eclipse IDE for App Engine coding and debugging. The Google Plugin adds the following functionality to your Eclipse IDE:

- New project wizards to automatically set the framework for App Engine projects and web development projects leveraging the Google Web Toolkit (GWT)

- Debugging tools to debug App Engine and GWT applications using the local development server

- Deployment tools to migrate your App Engine applications to appspot.com

Installing the Java SDK

Although App Engine supports both Java 5 and Java 6 we recommend that you run the Java 6 libraries and JVM for compiling and testing your application, because the Google App Engine production environment runs Java 6. So, naturally, you'll want to test and debug your application on the same platform that it will be running.

The fastest and easiest way to develop, debug, and deploy Java applications for App Engine is by using the Eclipse IDE and the Google Plugin for Eclipse. In the next section, we'll walk through the installation of the Eclipse IDE (Galileo) and the Google Plugin for Eclipse. Mac and Windows use the same installation process, and Figure 3-1 shows the installation dialog for both environments.

Installing the Google Plugin for Eclipse

Before you can install the Google Plugin for Eclipse you should verify that Java is running on your machine. (If you're already developing in Eclipse you can skip this step. Eclipse requires a JDK to function, so you're covered.) If you're installing Eclipse for the first time, verify that you have a JDK installed by running either of the following commands from the terminal.

```
java -version
javac - version
```

If you need to download a JDK, start by downloading the appropriate release from http://java.sun.com/javase/downloads. Follow the instructions to install the JDK, and then run the preceding commands again to verify that everything is set up correctly.

The Google Plugin for Eclipse is available for versions 3.3 (Europa), 3.4 (Ganymede), and 3.5 (Galileo) of the Eclipse IDE. To install the Eclipse IDE on a Mac, you just navigate to www.eclipse.org and download the distribution for Mac OS X. You need to extract a tar.gz file to the directory from which you'd like to run Eclipse, for example, the Documents folder on a Mac. You can choose any location; it won't have an affect on the exercises in this book.

Once you have the Eclipse IDE installed you can use the Software Update feature to install the Google Plugin for Eclipse. The Software Update feature is used to install common add-ons and third-party packages into your Eclipse environment. You can get started by launching Eclipse. On the Mac, double-click the file called Eclipse in the directory where you extracted the distribution.

To install the plug-in using Eclipse 3.5 (Galileo) (see Figure 3-1):

1. Select the Help menu and then select the Install New Software option.

2. In the Work with text box, enter **http://dl.google.com/eclipse/ plugin/3.5**.

3. Expand the "Plugin" and "SDKs" elements in the navigation tree. Select "Google Plugin for Eclipse 3.5" and "Google App Engine SDK". You'll use the Google Web Toolkit for some examples later in the book, so make sure you select the "Google Web Toolkit SDK" option as well. Click Next.

4. Restart Eclipse when prompted. Make sure you are using the Java perspective.

To install the plug-in, using Eclipse 3.4 (Ganymede):

1. Select the Help menu, and then select the Software Updates option.

2. Select the Available Software tab and click the Add Site button. In the Location text box enter **http://dl.google.com/eclipse/plugin/3.4**.

3. Expand the "Google" element in the navigation tree. Select "Google Plugin for Eclipse 3.4" and "Google App Engine Java SDK". You'll use the Google Web Toolkit for some examples later in the book, so make sure you select the "Google Web Toolkit SDK" option as well. Click Next. Follow the prompts to accept the terms of service and install the plug-in.

4. Restart Eclipse when prompted. Make sure you are using the Java perspective.

■ **Note** Eclipse 3.4 takes quite a bit longer to load then 3.5. That's because Eclipse checks for updates for all the plug-ins' dependencies. If you want to prevent Eclipse from checking all the dependencies, ensure that only Google Plugin for Eclipse 3.4 is selected in the Help ➤ Software Updates ➤ Available Software ➤ Manage Sites dialog.

Figure 3-1 shows the dialog for Mac, and Figure 3-2 shows the dialog for Windows versions of Eclipse 3.5 while selecting the Google Plugin for Eclipse options from the Add Software dialog.

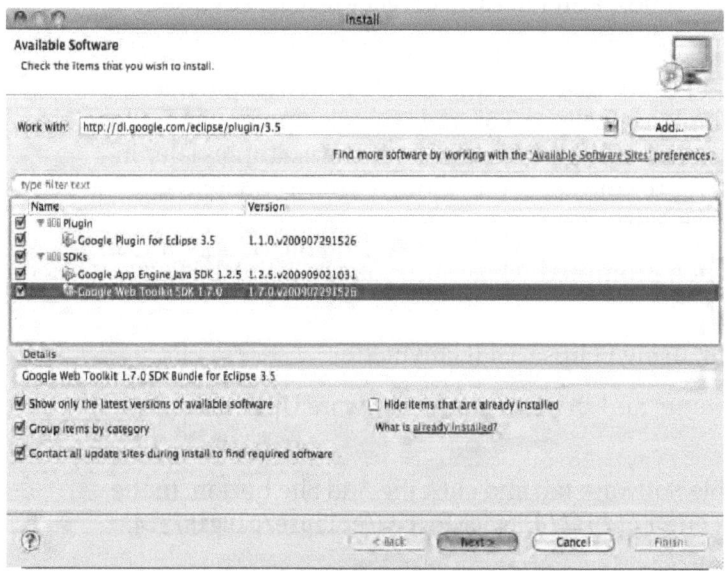

Figure 3-1. *Installing the Google Plugin for Eclipse on a Mac (Galileo)*

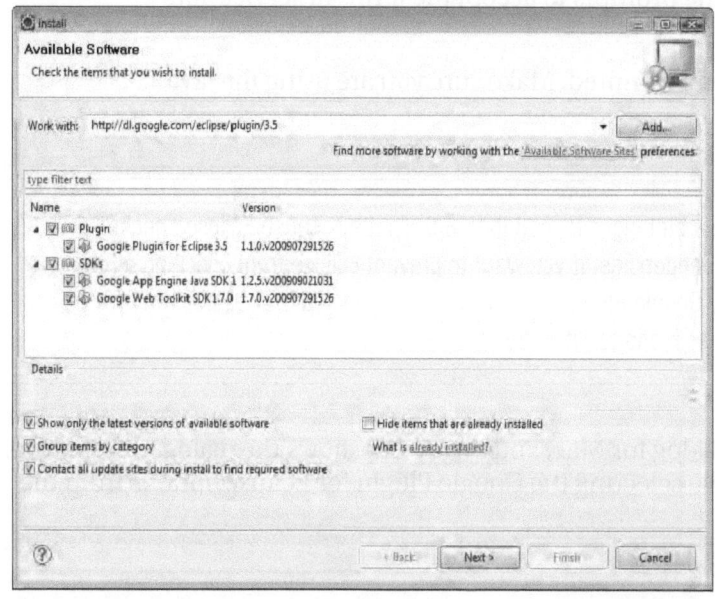

Figure 3-2. *Installing the Google Plugin for Eclipse on Windows (Galileo)*

Signing Up for Google App Engine

Before you get too far, you need to enable your Google account for access to App Engine. To get started, navigate to http://appengine.google.com. You'll be prompted for your Google account credentials, and you'll be asked to accept the terms of service. That's it! You're ready to get started, by launching the sample project that was installed with the SDK. If you don't have a Google account, you can register for one for free by browsing to https://www.google.com/accounts/NewAccount.

Launching the Demo Application

The App Engine Java SDK includes a few demo applications to help you get up and running. These might be a bit hard to locate. If you're new to Eclipse, it's important to note that all the SDKs and add-ons you install to your Eclipse environment get bundled in the plug-ins directory where you extracted the Eclipse distribution. In your case, the demo files for Google App Engine for Java will be located in the plugins/com.google.appengine.eclipse.sdk. [sdkbundle_VERSION/ directory, where VERSION is the version identifier of the SDK. There should be a demo directory under the subdirectory called "appengine-java-sdk-version". The online documentation for Google App Engine for Java walks you through the steps to create a guestbook application. You'll be creating your own application throughout the course of this book. However, to verify that you have set up your SDK correctly, open the precompiled demo application called Guestbook. This represents the final version of the guestbook application if you were to follow the online tutorials. Take a look around the application. We'll be walking through the creation of some of these features when you build your own application. To launch the application select Debug As ➤ Web Application from the Run menu in Eclipse.

Note that the authentication framework is present to facilitate local development with test accounts, as shown in Figure 3-3. If you click the Sign in link, you'll be forwarded to a basic login page asking for only your username. The local session will use whatever e-mail address you enter as the active user. If you'd like to log in with administrator privileges, make sure you check the "Sign in as Administrator" checkbox. The local development server that comes with the Google App Engine SDK provides a set of methods that generate sign-in and sign-out URLs and simulate Google accounts.

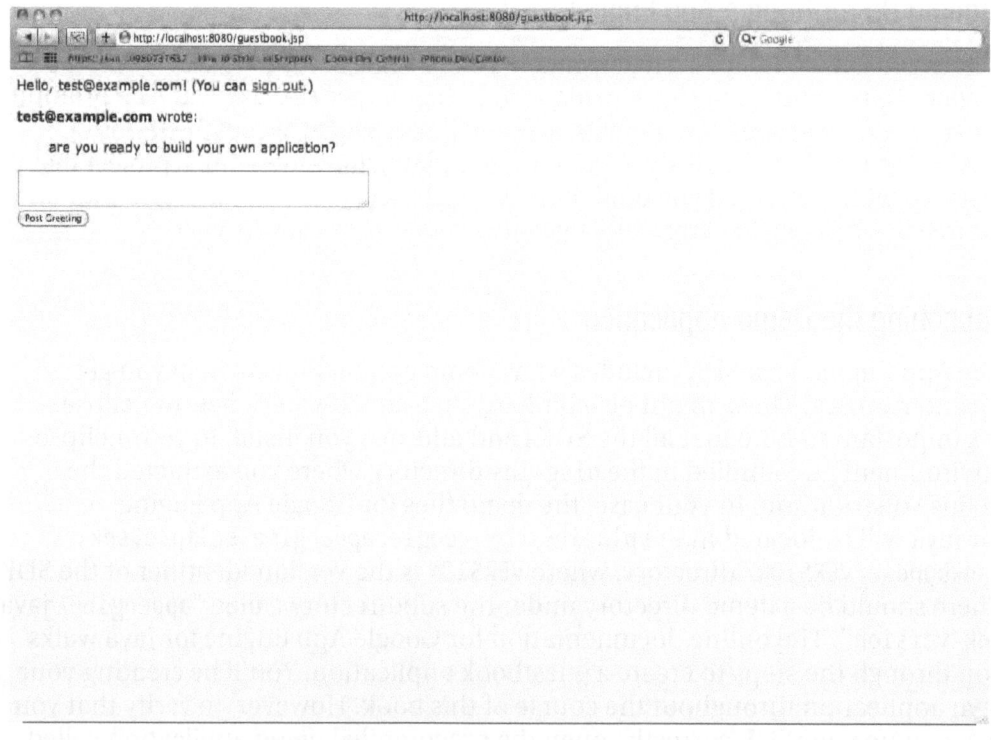

Figure 3-3. *The running guestbook demo application*

Create Your First App Engine Project

Now you'll create an App Engine project so you can get a deeper look at the structure and components that make up the project and some features of the local development server. Hopefully, you still have Eclipse open from the installation steps you just completed. If not, open Eclipse and make sure you are in the Java perspective. You should see Java (default) in the top-right corner of your Eclipse environment. You can select Java (default) from the Open Perspective menu after choosing Window on the toolbar. From the File menu choose New ➤ Web Application Project. Use the values described in Table 3-1 for your project.

Table 3-1. New Project Properties

Field	Value
Project Name	GAEJ - ChapterThree
Package	gaej.chapterthree
Location	Create new project in workspace
Google SDKs	Select both Google Web Toolkit and Google App Engine, and then select the default SDK for both. Yours may be a different version from that shown in Figure 3-4.

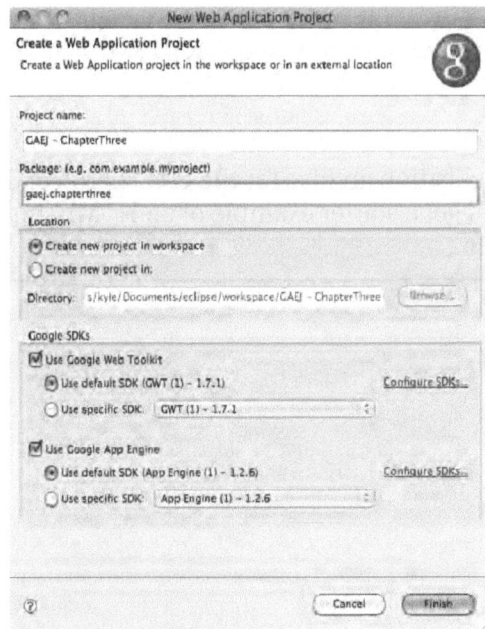

Figure 3-4. The New Web Application Project wizard

Project Artifacts

Since you are using the Google Web Toolkit for this application, you'll get a starter template called the Guest-Service application. You'll examine the project assets and learn how to compile, run, and deploy your test application. You can see from Figure 3-5 that a decent number of artifacts were loaded with your new project. Table 3-2 gives you a look at what each one of these artifacts does.

Table 3-2. *New Project Properties*

Artifact	Purpose
src/gaej.chaptertwo[GAEJ___ChapterThree.gwt.xml]	A GWT Module descriptor that loads the settings for GWT in this application. You can set things like the GWT theme and the application entry points here.
src/gaej.chaptertwo.server[GreetingServiceImpl.java]	The server-side implementation of the GreetingService.
src/gaej.chaptertwo.client[GAEJ___ChapterThree.java][GreetingService.java][GreetingServiceAsync.java]	This includes the main entry point for the application as well as the code for the Synchronous and Asynchronous API for the GreetingService.
War[WEB-INF/web.xml][GAEJ___ChapterThree.html][GAEJ___ChatperThree.css]	The web application archive for the GAE/J project. By default you'll get a starter example of an HTML shell and a CSS file.

Figure 3-5. *Default project artifacts for the GWT / GAE/J project*

Before we start dissecting the code, it's important to look at what the starter application does. To launch the application from within Eclipse you can either right-click the project and select Run as ➤ Web Application or choose Web Application from the Run menu. Because you are using GWT for this project, the GWT Hosted Mode Console will launch when you run or debug the application. The application will prompt you for your name, as shown in Figure 3-6. Click Send and you should see something similar to Figure 3-7.

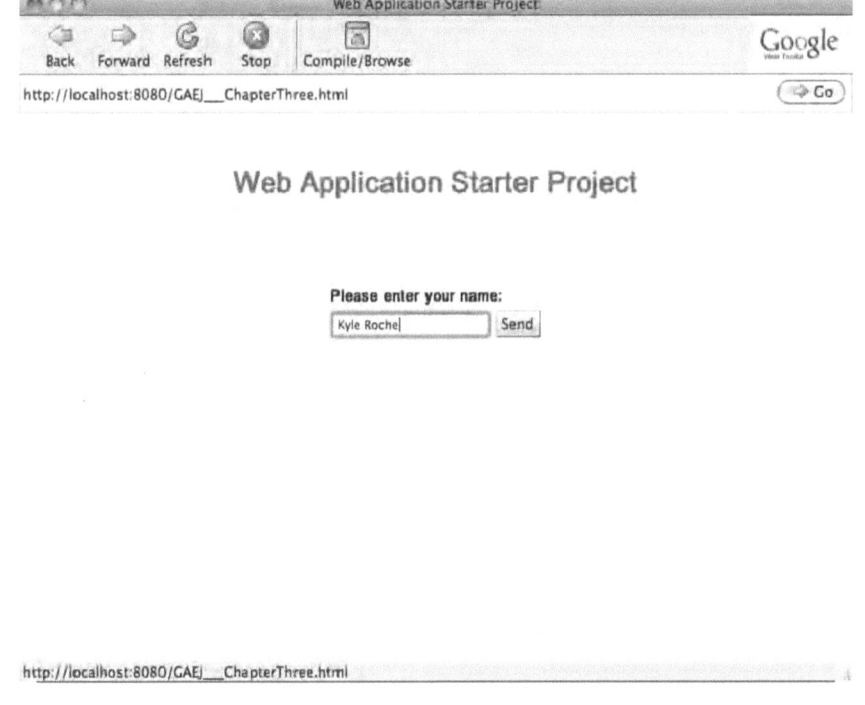

Figure 3-6. *Web Application Starter Project (GWT)*

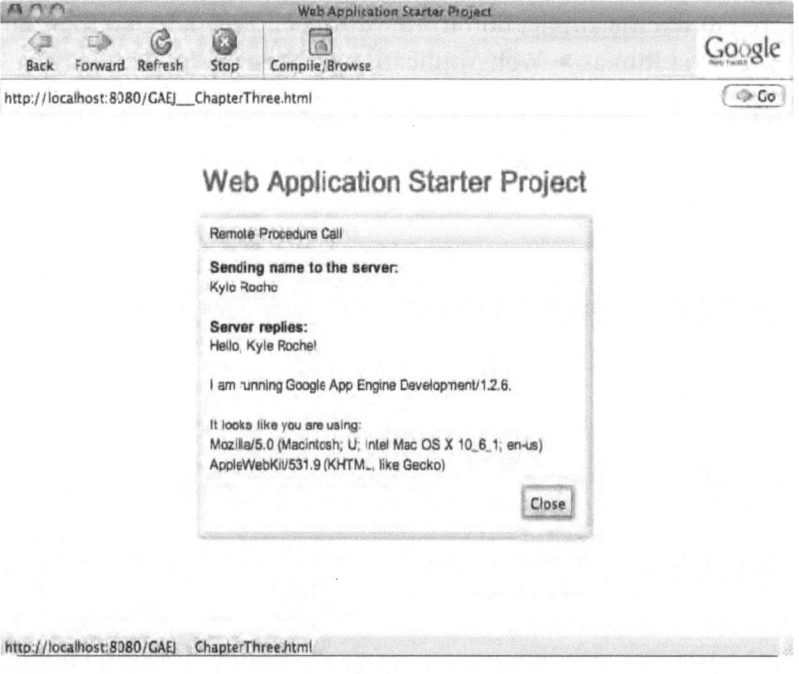

Figure 3-7. *Web Application Starter Project (GWT)*

Close the GWT Hosted Browser and return to Eclipse. Open the
GAEJ___ChapterThree.gwt.xml file from under the src/gaej.chaptertwo element
in the Package Explorer navigation tree. You should see the module XML element in
the Source view of the file, as shown in Listing 3-1.

Listing 3-1. *Module XML Element*

```
<module rename-to='gaej___chapterthree'>
  <!-- Inherit the core Web Toolkit stuff. -->
  <inherits name='com.google.gwt.user.User'/>

  <!-- Inherit the default GWT style sheet.  You can change     -->
  <!-- the theme of your GWT application by uncommenting         -->
  <!-- any one of the following lines.                           -->
  <inherits name='com.google.gwt.user.theme.standard.Standard'/>
  <!-- <inherits name='com.google.gwt.user.theme.chrome.Chrome'/> -->
  <!-- <inherits name='com.google.gwt.user.theme.dark.Dark'/>     -->
```

```
<!-- Other module inherits                                    -->

<!-- Specify the app entry point class.                       -->
<entry-point class='gaej.chaptertwo.client.GAEJ___ChapterThree'/>
</module>
```

If you'd like to start playing around with the GWT options, you can comment out the following line:

```
<inherits name='com.google.gwt.user.theme.standard.Standard'/>
```

Then uncomment out either of these lines:

```
<!-- <inherits name='com.google.gwt.user.theme.chrome.Chrome'/> -->
<!-- <inherits name='com.google.gwt.user.theme.dark.Dark'/>      -->
```

That change instructs GWT to load a new CSS template for the Dark or Chrome theme. Dark is a more significant change from the Standard theme. You might not notice the change from Standard to Chrome with the minimal amount of GWT components in use in the starter application.

We need to point out another important setting in the file. That's the following line:

```
<entry-point class='gaej.chapterthree.client.GAEJ___ChapterThree'/>
```

That line tells App Engine where the entry point for the application is located. Find the GAEJ___ChapterThree.java file under the src/gaej.chapterthree.client element in the Package Explorer. There are a few key methods to browse to get an idea of what's going on with the sample application. Look for the onModuleLoad() method. It should look similar to the code in Listing 3-2.

Listing 3-2. *Code for the onModuleLoad() method*

```
public void onModuleLoad() {
final Button sendButton = new Button("Send");
      final TextBox nameField = new TextBox();
      nameField.setText("GWT User");

      // We can add style names to widgets
      sendButton.addStyleName("sendButton");
```

```
            // Add the nameField and sendButton to the RootPanel
            // Use RootPanel.get() to get the entire body element
            RootPanel.get("nameFieldContainer").add(nameField);
            RootPanel.get("sendButtonContainer").add(sendButton);

            // Focus the cursor on the name field when the app loads
            nameField.setFocus(true);
            nameField.selectAll();

            // Create the popup dialog box
            final DialogBox dialogBox = new DialogBox();
            dialogBox.setText("Remote Procedure Call");
            dialogBox.setAnimationEnabled(true);
            final Button closeButton = new Button("Close");
            // We can set the id of a widget by accessing its Element
            closeButton.getElement().setId("closeButton");
            final Label textToServerLabel = new Label();
            final HTML serverResponseLabel = new HTML();
            VerticalPanel dialogVPanel = new VerticalPanel();
            dialogVPanel.addStyleName("dialogVPanel");
            dialogVPanel.add(new HTML("<b>Sending name to the server:</b>"));
            dialogVPanel.add(textToServerLabel);
            dialogVPanel.add(new HTML("<br><b>Server replies:</b>"));
            dialogVPanel.add(serverResponseLabel);
            dialogVPanel.setHorizontalAlignment(VerticalPanel.ALIGN_RIGHT);
            dialogVPanel.add(closeButton);
            dialogBox.setWidget(dialogVPanel);

            // Add a handler to close the DialogBox
            closeButton.addClickHandler(new ClickHandler() {

public void onClick(ClickEvent event) {
                dialogBox.hide();
                sendButton.setEnabled(true);
                sendButton.setFocus(true);
        }
    });
```

Without ever even using GWT you can quickly browse the code and follow exactly what is happening. The method loads the Google Web Toolkit elements in an order and fashion that lays out your page perfectly. Take the following lines, for example.

```
RootPanel.get("nameFieldContainer").add(nameField);
RootPanel.get("sendButtonContainer").add(sendButton);
```

If you open the GAEJ___ChapterThree.html file from the web application archive (war directory) you can see the following HTML elements.

```
<td id="nameFieldContainer"></td>
<td id="sendButtonContainer"></td>
```

GWT, using the add() method of the RootPanel class, knows to insert the GWT components in that section of the application's HTML. You can see how quickly and easily you can leverage the power of Google Web Toolkit to build a pretty impressive application.

Local Development Server

The App Engine SDK comes with a local development server for App Engine testing and debugging. This is required because the Java Runtime on App Engine is slightly different from the standard distribution. For example, you can't open ports or sockets in App Engine. To make a remote HTTP request you need to implement App Engine's URL Fetch service (covered in Chapter 8). The development server is part of the SDK. You can't use your own development server for App Engine debugging and testing. The App Engine JRE differs from other implementations. Let's take a deeper look at some of the features of the local development server and some miscellaneous tools to accelerate application development on App Engine.

Ready to Launch

Soon after the birth of App Engine, a few Google employees used their "20 percent time" (one day a week to work on projects that may not be part of their official jobs) to create an App Engine launcher for Mac. With the release of the App Engine 1.2.5 SDK there was a second group of 20-percenters that released a Windows/Linux version of the launcher. The source code for all these distributions is available at code.google.com.

Figure 3-8 shows the App Engine Launcher for Mac. The launcher helps you edit the configuration files for both Python and Java App Engine projects, browse your applications locally, and even deploy your applications to the production environment. If you're interested, the source code for the Mac launcher is located here on Google Code: `http://code.google.com/p/google-appengine-mac-launcher`.

■ **Note** Google Suggest, AdSense for Content, and Orkut are among the many products created through the "20 percent time" perk.

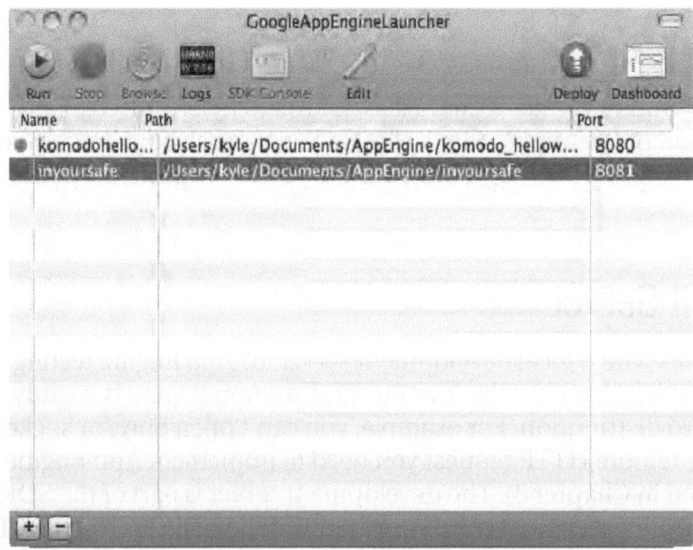

Figure 3-8. *The Google App Engine launcher for Mac*

You don't have to use the launcher to start your development projects on the local development server. If you're using Eclipse and the Google Eclipse Plugin, you can launch your application locally by selecting Debug As ➤ Web Application from the Run menu.

For more control or to script the launch of your applications locally, you can launch the development web server from the command line. You should execute this command from the SDK's appengine-java-sdk/bin directory.

If you are using Windows, run the following command:

```
appengine-java-sdk\bin\dev_appserver.cmd [options] war-location
```

If you are using Mac OS X or Linux, run the following command:

```
appengine-java-sdk/bin/dev_appserver.sh [options] war-location
```

These commands are OS-specific wrapper scripts that run the Java class com.google.appengine.tools.KickStart in appengine-java-sdk/lib/appengine-tools-api.jar. For details on the available command options reference the online documentation.

■ **Note** To stop the development server, press Control + C (on Windows, Mac, or Linux).

Deploying Your Sample Application

It's time to deploy your application to App Engine where you can browse it publicly and share it with the world. There's a small Jet Engine icon in your Eclipse tool bar that was created when you installed the Google Eclipse Plugin. Click that icon while making sure that your ChapterThree sample application is selected in the Package Explorer. It's important to note that, at the time of this writing, you get 10 applications per account. You may consider choosing generic application IDs for the examples in this book and reusing them for each chapter.

You'll be presented with a Deploy Project to Google App Engine dialog like the one shown in Figure 3-9. The project name should have been defaulted to the project you had selected in Eclipse. If it's blank or doesn't look quite right, click cancel, select the ChapterThree project in Eclipse, and click the Jet Engine button again.

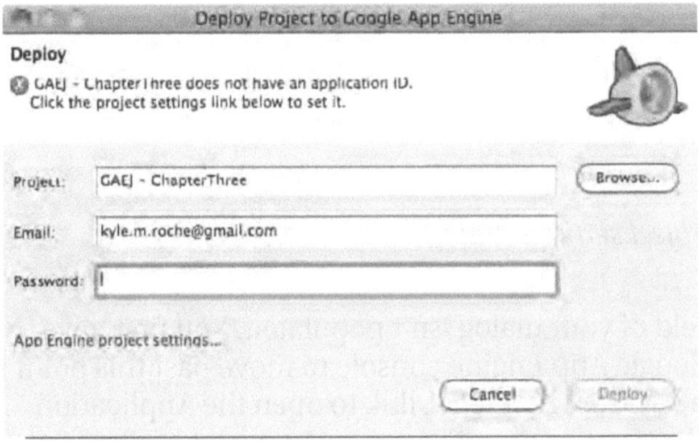

Figure 3-9. The Deploy Project to Google App Engine dialog

Once you're ready to move forward click the App Engine project settings... link at the bottom of the dialog window. You'll see something similar to Figure 3-10.

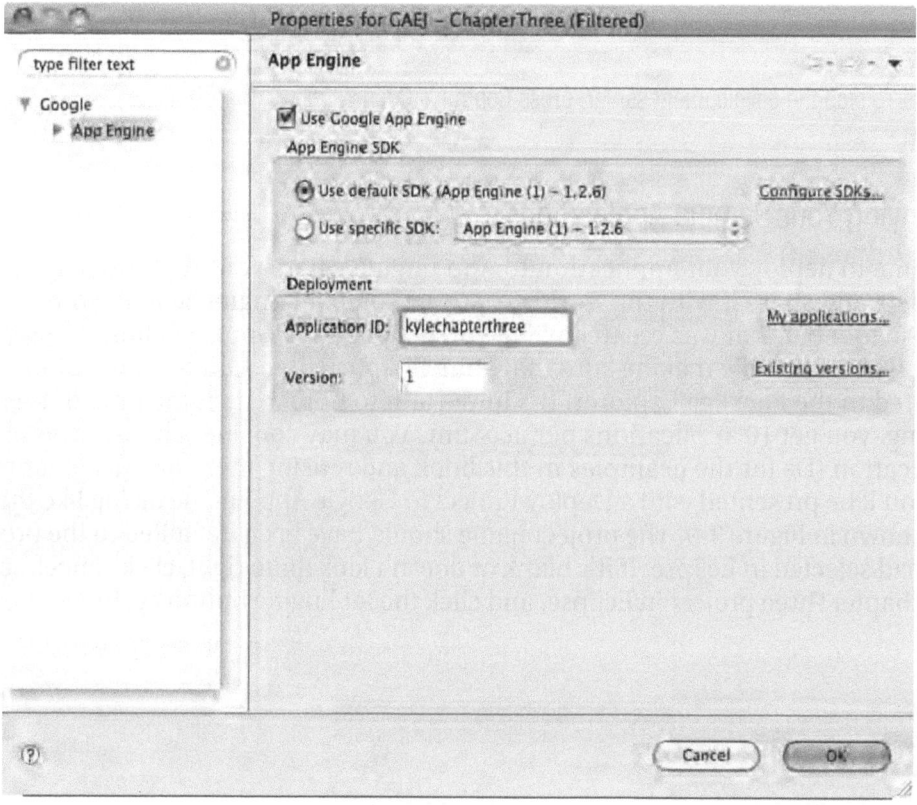

Figure 3-10. *The App Engine project settings dialog*

Note that the Application ID field of your dialog isn't populated. You first have to create the application in your Google App Engine console to move past this point in the deployment process. Use the My applications... link to open the Application Registration form for your App Engine account. Figures 3-11 and 3-12 follow the process for your account. You'll have to create a unique Application identifier, which must be unique across the appspot.com domain. Use the Check Availability feature to verify that your application ID is available.

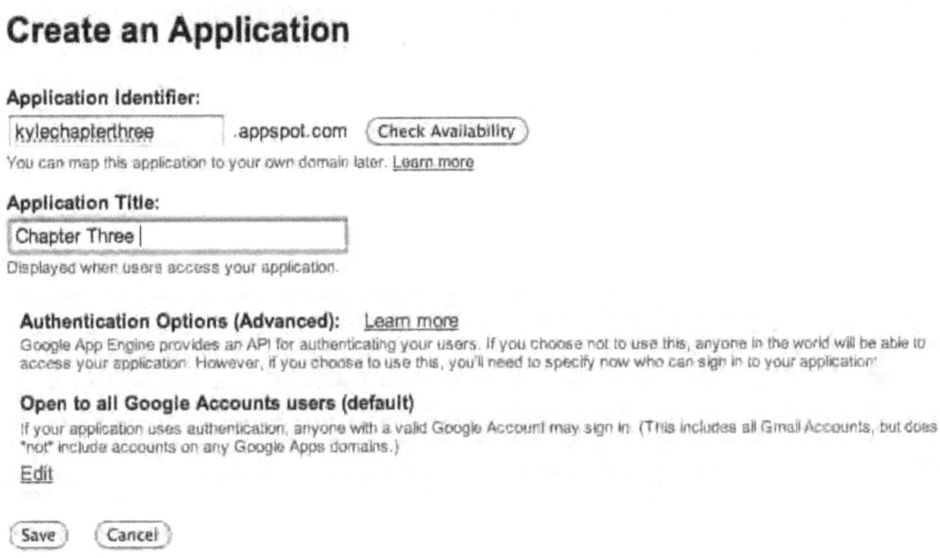

Create an Application

Application Identifier:

kylechapterthree   .appspot.com   (Check Availability)

You can map this application to your own domain later. Learn more

Application Title:

Chapter Three |

Displayed when users access your application.

Authentication Options (Advanced):   Learn more

Google App Engine provides an API for authenticating your users. If you choose not to use this, anyone in the world will be able to access your application. However, if you choose to use this, you'll need to specify now who can sign in to your application:

Open to all Google Accounts users (default)

If your application uses authentication, anyone with a valid Google Account may sign in. (This includes all Gmail Accounts, but does *not* include accounts on any Google Apps domains.)

Edit

(Save)   (Cancel)

Figure 3-11. Registering kylechapterthree.appspot.com (use a unique name)

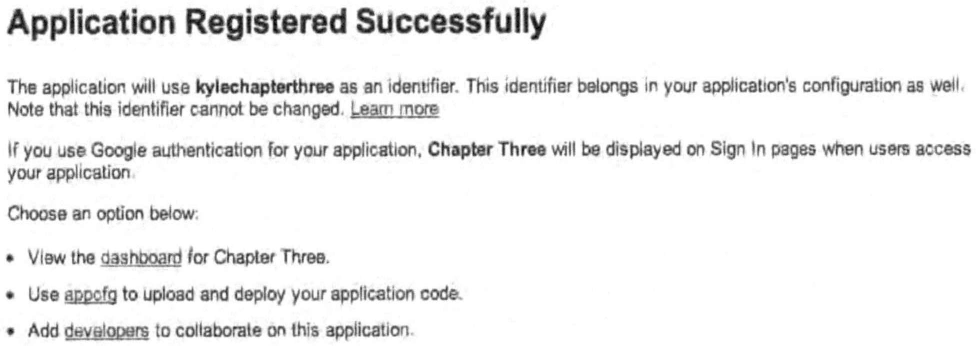

Application Registered Successfully

The application will use **kylechapterthree** as an identifier. This identifier belongs in your application's configuration as well. Note that this identifier cannot be changed. Learn more

If you use Google authentication for your application, **Chapter Three** will be displayed on Sign In pages when users access your application.

Choose an option below:

- View the dashboard for Chapter Three.
- Use appcfg to upload and deploy your application code.
- Add developers to collaborate on this application.

Figure 3-12. Confirming that the application was registered

Now that you've deployed your application you have a few options for production use. You can browse to your application live on appspot.com by navigating to your application's unique domain on appspot. In the example case (shown in Figures 3-11 and 3-12), the application lives at http://kylechapterthree.appspot.com, as shown in

Figure 3-13. If you're using Google Apps you can create a unique domain name for your App Engine application. We'll look at that later in the book.

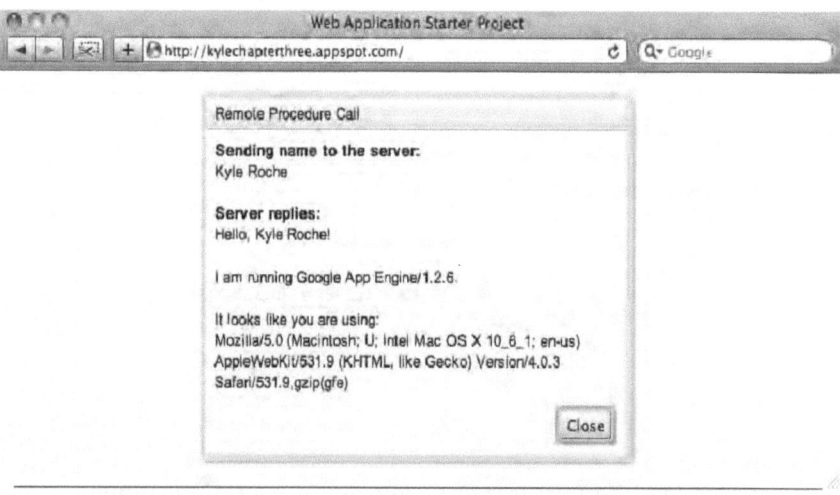

Figure 3-13. *The application live on appspot.com*

Summary

In this chapter you built your first Google App Engine for Java application using the Guestbook demo application that comes with the SDK. You set up and configured the SDK and Google Plugin for Eclipse and even deployed your application to appspot.com. We're going to dive a little deeper into some development technologies and application components in Chapter 4, where you'll look at different approaches to constructing a user interface in an App Engine application and review some libraries and development frameworks.

CHAPTER 4

■■■

Servlet Container and Frameworks

Now that you've set up your development environment and configured the SDK, it's time to look at the design of your application. Out of the box, App Engine uses the Java Servlet standard for web applications, but you may be able to use your favorite framework as well. In this chapter we'll look at different libraries and frameworks that run in App Engine. You'll build a small application with servlets and JavaServer (JSP) pages as well as applications using Spring MVC and Adobe Flex with GraniteDS.

Choosing a Framework

Choosing the best application framework almost always generates a heated debate. There are pros and cons for each framework, and every developer has an opinion. Some developers may prefer a robust Enterprise JavaBeans (EJB) framework while others prefer a lightweight, agile approach. To ensure that your application will run within the App Engine server runtime environment, App Engine imposes some constraints that enable applications to run "nicely" together and be scalable across multiple distributed runtime instances.

While Google doesn't officially support the libraries or frameworks that run on App Engine, it does take a community-oriented approach to compatibility. While many frameworks will run seamlessly on App Engine, others will not. Some frameworks will require modifications, and there is an active and vibrant community dedicated to interoperability.

Popular Java libraries and frameworks are listed in Table 4-1. Frameworks marked as compatible should work out-of-the-box with some minor configuration changes or code tweaks. Ones marked "Semi-compatible" typically include some features that will not operate properly due to App Engine restrictions (for example, writing to the file system, multithreading). Most incompatible frameworks fail to run due to their reliance on classes not supported by App Engine.

Table 4-1. *Java libraries and frameworks from Google's "Will it play in App Engine" page*

Framework	Version(s)	Status
Apache Commons FileUpload	1.2.1	Semi-Compatible
Apache POI	?	Incompatible
BlazeDS	3.2.0	Compatible
Compass	?	Semi-Compatible
Direct Web Remoting (DWR)	2.0.5, 3.0 RC1	Compatible
dyuproject	?	Compatible
Ehcache	1.6.0	Compatible
Facelets	1.1.14	Compatible
Google Data (GData) client library for Java	All	Compatible
Grails	1.1.1	Compatible
GraniteDS	?	Compatible
Guice	?	Semi-Compatible
Hibernate	All	Incompatible
iText	?	Incompatible
Java Topology Suite (JTS)	1.10	Compatible
JBoss Seam	?	Semi-Compatible
Jersey	1.0.2	Semi-Compatible
log4j	?	Compatible

Framework	Version(s)	Status
MyFaces	1.1.6	Compatible
OpenSocial client library for Java	20090402	Compatible
OSGi	?	Semi-Compatible
Restlet	?	Compatible
RichFaces	3.1.6	Incompatible
SiteMesh	2.4.2 +	Compatible
Spring MVC	2.5.6	Compatible
Spring ORM	2.5.6	Compatible
Spring Security	?	Semi-Compatible
Stripes Framework	?	Compatible
Struts 1	1.2.28	Compatible
Struts 2	?	Compatible
Tapestry	5.0.18	Compatible
Tapestry	5.1	Incompatible
Tiles	2.0.7	Compatible
Vaadin	?	Semi-Compatible
VRaptor 2	?	Compatible
WebORB	?	Compatible
Wicket	?	Semi-Compatible
ZK	3.6.2 +	Compatible

Depending on your application's needs, you may or may not choose to use a framework. You can certainly develop feature-rich, scalable applications for App Engine using servlets and JSPs. We are going to take a quick peek at some applications built using the Java Servlet standard, Swing MVC, and Adobe Flex with GraniteDS.

Servlets and JavaServer Pages

For web applications, the Java Servlet standard is one of the major foundations of the server stack. By default App Engine utilizes this tried-and-true standard for web applications as well. As with most servlet containers, App Engine serves up servlets, JSPs, static files, and other data files from the web archive (WAR) directory based on the configuration in the deployment descriptor. Gone are the days of manually configuring and load-balancing your servers based on traffic. A major advantage of App Engine is that it automatically scales your application for you. Applications run on multiple web servers simultaneously and Google automatically adjusts the server pool based on the load.

As with most multitenant environments, App Engine runs the JVM in a secured "sandbox" environment to isolate applications from one another for security and service availability. The sandbox ensures that applications don't step on one another, hog server resources, or perform actions that they shouldn't. These restrictions can be great for ensuring scalability but can make you want to pull your hair out sometimes. For instance, applications don't have access to the local file system for write operations, cannot spawn threads, cannot leverage JNI or other native code, and cannot make ad hoc network connections. Most of the time it's not an issue, but in certain cases you'll find yourself wanting to write to the local file system or spawn a new thread to perform operations more efficiently.

To get started with App Engine, you're going to build a small application that incorporates some basic functionality. The application is a simple telesales application that sales representatives can use to field inbound sales calls. Users will be able to search for existing accounts or create new accounts. They can view existing sales opportunities for the account or create new opportunities that other sales reps can follow up on. Your application will contain a single servlet and a number of JSPs. You'll persist your data to Bigtable. (We'll just skim over the functionality here, as we'll dig into Bigtable in detail in Chapter 7.)

Views

Starting with the views for your application, the servlet container serves a welcome page (Figure 4-1 and Listing 4-1), a simple form that allows the user to perform a keyword search for existing accounts in Bigtable. Users can also choose to create a new account for sales opportunities.

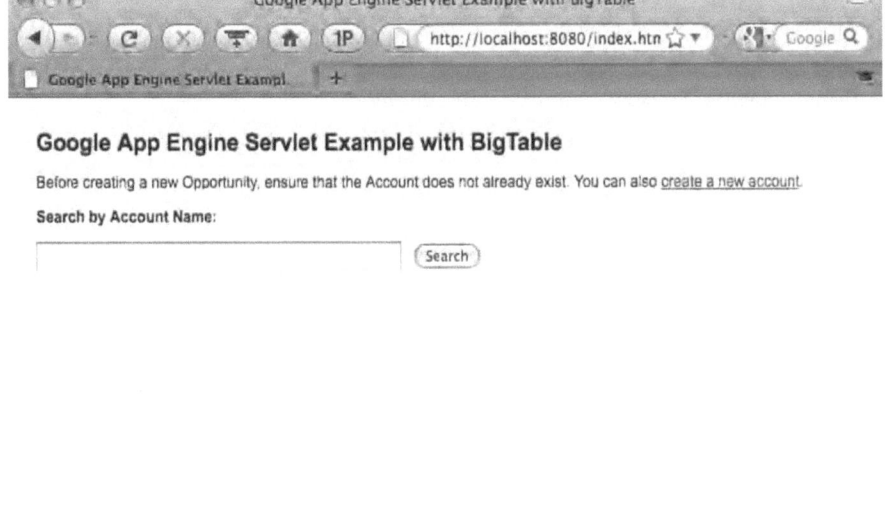

Figure 4-1. *The default welcome web page*

Listing 4-1. *The code for index.html*

```
<html>
<head>
      <title>Google App Engine Servlet Example with Bigtable</title>
      <link rel="stylesheet" type="text/css"
href="/stylesheets/styles.css"/>
</head>
<body>
      <span class="title">Google App Engine Servlet Example with
Bigtable</span>
      <p>Before creating a new Opportunity, ensure that the Account does
not already exist. You can also <a
href="telesales?action=accountCreate"/>create a new account</a>.</p>
      <p/>
      <form method="post" action="telesales">
```

```
            <input type="hidden" name="action" value="accountLookup"/>
            <span class="heading">Search by Account Name:</span>
            <p/>
            <input type="text" name="accountName" value="ACME"
style="width: 300px"/>
             
            <input type="submit" value="Search"/>
             
      </form>
      <p/>

</body>
</html>
```

If the account does not exist, users can create a new account using a standard HTML form, as shown in Figure 4-2. You are simply collecting some summary information in order to identify the account. Listing 4-2 contains the code for your input form.

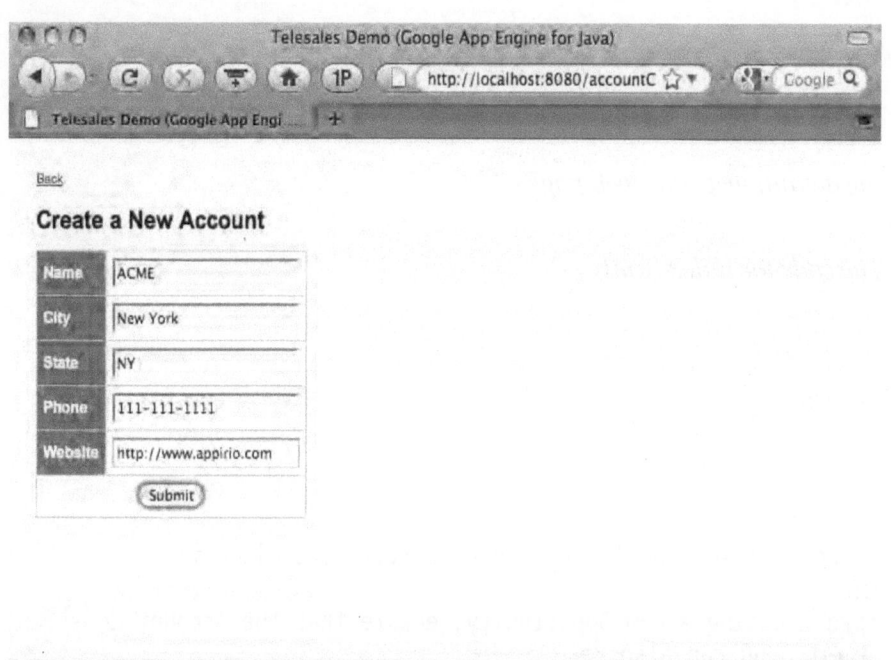

Figure 4-2. The Create a New Account web page

Listing 4-2. The code for accountCreate.jsp

```html
<html>
<head>
      <title>Telesales Demo (Google App Engine for Java)</title>
      <link rel="stylesheet" type="text/css"
href="/stylesheets/styles.css"/>
</head>
<body>
      <span class="nav"><a href="index.html">Back</a></span><p/>
      <span class="title">Create a New Account</span>
      <p/>

      <form method="get" action="telesales">
      <input type="hidden" name="action" value="accountCreateDo"/>
      <table border="0" cellspacing="1" cellpadding="5" bgcolor="#CCCCCC">
            <tr bgcolor="#407BA8">
                  <td style="color: #ffffff; font-weight: bold;">Name</td>
                  <td bgcolor="#ffffff"><input type="input"
name="name"></td>
            </tr>
            <tr bgcolor="#407BA8">
                  <td style="color: #ffffff; font-weight: bold;">City</td>
                  <td bgcolor="#ffffff"><input type="input"
name="billingCity"></td>
            </tr>
            <tr bgcolor="#407BA8">
                  <td style="color: #ffffff; font-weight:
bold;">State</td>
                  <td bgcolor="#ffffff"><input type="input"
name="billingState"></td>
            </tr>
            <tr bgcolor="#407BA8">
                  <td style="color: #ffffff; font-weight:
bold;">Phone</td>
                  <td bgcolor="#ffffff"><input type="input"
name="phone"></td>
            </tr>
            <tr bgcolor="#407BA8">
                  <td style="color: #ffffff; font-weight:
bold;">Website</td>
```

```
                        <td bgcolor="#ffffff"><input type="input"
name="website"></td>
            </tr>
            <tr>
                <td colspan="2" bgcolor="#ffffff" align="center"><input
type="submit" value="Submit"></td>
            </tr>
        </table>
        </form>

</body>
</html>
```

The search results page (Figure 4-3) displays the accounts returned from the servlet. Listing 4-3 contains the code to display the search box and any results returned from Bigtable by the keyword search. Users can click the account name to obtain more details about the account.

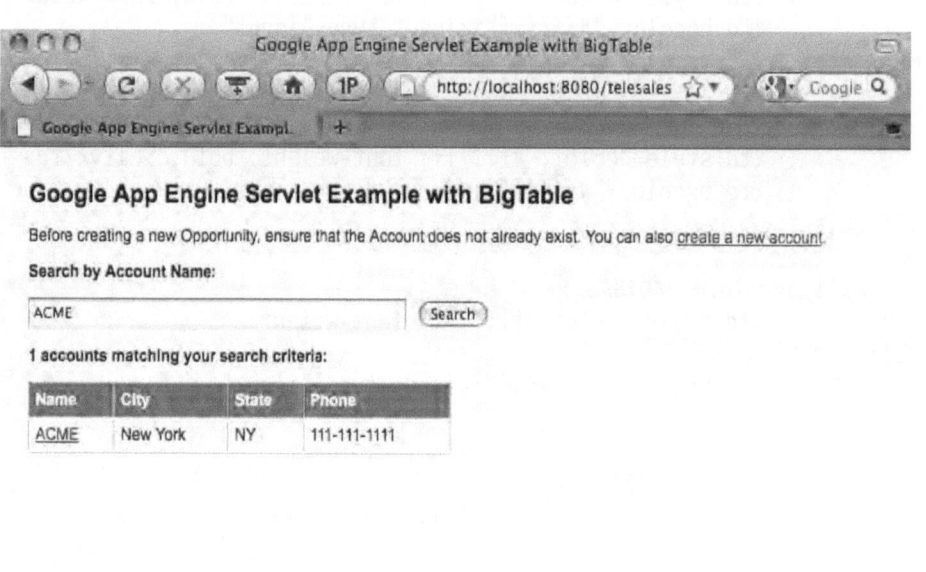

Figure 4-3. *The account lookup web page*

Listing 4-3. *The code for accountLookup.jsp*

```jsp
<%@ page import="java.util.List"%>
<%@ page import="com.appirio.entity.*"%>

<%
    List<Account> accounts =
(List<Account>)request.getAttribute("accounts");
%>

<html>
<head>
    <title>Google App Engine Servlet Example with Bigtable</title>
    <link rel="stylesheet" type="text/css"
href="/stylesheets/styles.css"/>
</head>
<body>
    <span class="title">Google App Engine Servlet Example with
Bigtable</span>
    <p/>
    <p>Before creating a new Opportunity, ensure that the Account does
not already exist. You can also <a
href="telesales?action=accountCreate"/>create a new account</a>.</p>
    <p/>
    <form method="post" action="telesales">
        <input type="hidden" name="action" value="accountLookup"/>
        <span class="heading">Search by Account Name:</span>
        <p/>
        <input type="text" name="accountName" value="<% if
(request.getParameter("accountName") != null) {
out.println(request.getParameter("accountName")); } %>" style="width:
300px"/>
         
        <input type="submit" value="Search"/>
         
    </form>
    <p/>
    <% if (accounts.size() > 0) { %>
        <span class="heading"><%= accounts.size() %> accounts matching
your search criteria:</span>

        <p/>
```

```
                <table border="0" cellspacing="1" cellpadding="5"
bgcolor="#CCCCCC" width="50%">
                <tr bgcolor="#407BA8">
                    <td style="color: #ffffff; font-weight: bold;">Name</td>
                    <td style="color: #ffffff; font-weight: bold;">City</td>
                    <td style="color: #ffffff; font-weight:
bold;">State</td>
                    <td style="color: #ffffff; font-weight:
bold;">Phone</td>
                </tr>
                <% for (int i = 0;i<accounts.size();i++) { %>
                    <% Account a = (Account)accounts.get(i); %>
                    <tr style="background:#ffffff"
onMouseOver="this.style.background='#eeeeee';"
onMouseOut="this.style.background='#ffffff';">
                        <td><a
href="telesales?action=accountDisplay&accountId=<%= a.getId() %>"><%=
a.getName() %></a></td>
                        <td><%= a.getCity() %></td>
                        <td><%= a.getState() %></td>
                        <td><%= a.getPhone() %></td>
                    </tr>
                <% } %>
                </table>

        <% } else { %>
                <span class="heading">No matching accounts found.</span>
        <% } %>
        <p/>

</body>
</html>
```

The Account Display view (Figure 4-4) shows the details of the account, a link to create a new sales opportunity, and a list of all opportunities for the account in Bigtable. Listing 4-4 contains the code for this page.

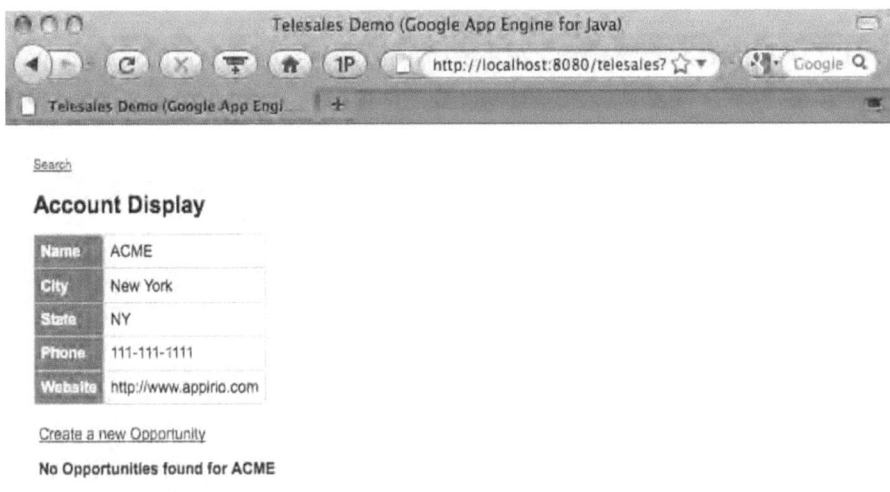

Figure 4-4. The Account Display web page

Listing 4-4. The code for accountDisplay.jsp

```jsp
<%@ page import="java.util.List"%>
<%@ page import="java.text.SimpleDateFormat"%>
<%@ page import="com.appirio.entity.*"%>

<%
    Account account = (Account)request.getAttribute("account");
    List<Opportunity> opportunities =
(List<Opportunity>)request.getAttribute("opportunities");
    SimpleDateFormat sdf = new SimpleDateFormat("M/d/yyyy");
%>

<html>
<head>
    <title>Telesales Demo (Google App Engine for Java)</title>
    <link rel="stylesheet" type="text/css"
href="/stylesheets/styles.css"/>
</head>
```

```
<body>
    <span class="nav"><a href="/index.html">Search</a></span><p/>
    <span class="title">Account Display</span>
    <p/>

    <table border="0" cellspacing="1" cellpadding="5" bgcolor="#CCCCCC">
        <tr bgcolor="#407BA8">
            <td style="color: #ffffff; font-weight: bold;">Name</td>
            <td bgcolor="#ffffff"><%= account.getName() %></td>
        </tr>
        <tr bgcolor="#407BA8">
            <td style="color: #ffffff; font-weight: bold;">City</td>
            <td bgcolor="#ffffff"><%= account.getCity() %></td>
        </tr>
        <tr bgcolor="#407BA8">
            <td style="color: #ffffff; font-weight:
bold;">State</td>
            <td bgcolor="#ffffff"><%= account.getState() %></td>
        </tr>
        <tr bgcolor="#407BA8">
            <td style="color: #ffffff; font-weight:
bold;">Phone</td>
            <td bgcolor="#ffffff"><%= account.getPhone() %></td>
        </tr>
        <tr bgcolor="#407BA8">
            <td style="color: #ffffff; font-weight:
bold;">Website</td>
            <td bgcolor="#ffffff"><%= account.getWebsite() %></td>
        </tr>
    </table>

    <br><a href="telesales?action=opportunityCreate&accountId=<%=
account.getId() %>">Create a new Opportunity</a><p/>

    <% if (opportunities.size() > 0) { %>

        <p/><span class="heading">Opportunities for <%=
account.getName() %></span><br><p/>

        <table border="0" cellspacing="1" cellpadding="5"
bgcolor="#CCCCCC">
            <tr bgcolor="#407BA8">
```

```
                    <td style="color: #ffffff; font-weight: bold;">Name</td>
                    <td style="color: #ffffff; font-weight:
bold;">Amount</td>
                    <td style="color: #ffffff; font-weight:
bold;">Stage</td>
                    <td style="color: #ffffff; font-weight:
bold;">Probability</td>
                    <td style="color: #ffffff; font-weight: bold;">Close
Date</td>
                    <td style="color: #ffffff; font-weight:
bold;">Order</td>
              </tr>
            <% for (int i = 0;i<opportunities.size();i++) { %>
                  <% Opportunity o = (Opportunity)opportunities.get(i); %>
                  <tr style="background:#ffffff"
onMouseOver="this.style.background='#eeeeee';"
onMouseOut="this.style.background='#ffffff';">
                        <td nowrap><%= o.getName() %></td>
                        <td>$<%= o.getAmount() %></td>
                        <td><%= o.getStageName() %></td>
                        <td><%= o.getProbability() %>%</td>
                        <td><%= sdf.format(o.getCloseDate()) %></td>
                        <td><%= o.getOrderNumber() %></td>
                  </tr>
            <% } %>
            </table>

      <% } else { %>
            <p/><span class="heading">No Opportunities found for <%=
account.getName() %></span>
      <% } %>

</body>
</html>
```

Listing 4-5 contains the code for the Create New Opportunity page, which is shown in Figure 4-5. This HTML form collects the name of the opportunity, the anticipated amount of the opportunity, and some additional attributes. Submitting the form creates the new opportunity in Bigtable and takes users back to the Account Display page where they can view the newly created opportunity (Figure 4-6).

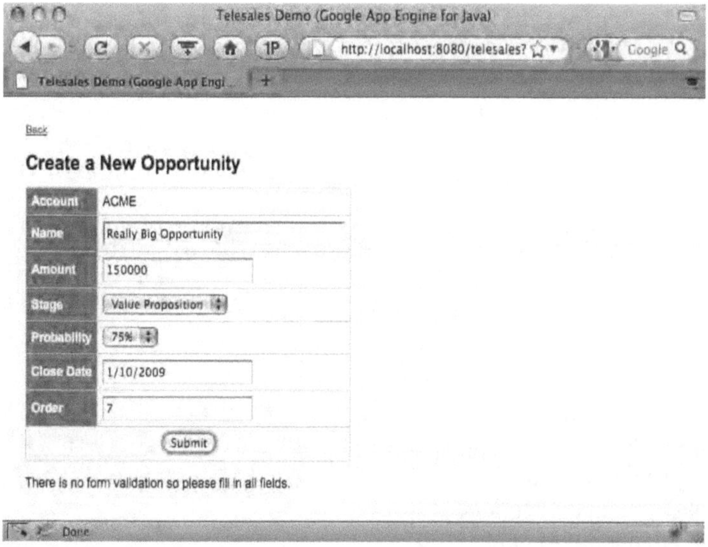

Figure 4-5. *The Create a New Opportunity web page*

Listing 4-5. *The code for opportunityCreate.jsp*

```
<%
        String accountName = (String)request.getAttribute("accountName");
%>

<html>
<head>
        <title>Telesales Demo (Google App Engine for Java)</title>
        <link rel="stylesheet" type="text/css"
href="/stylesheets/styles.css"/>
</head>
<body>
        <span class="nav"><a
href="telesales?action=accountDisplay&accountId=<%=
request.getParameter("accountId") %>">Back</a></span><p/>
        <span class="title">Create a New Opportunity</span>
        <p/>

        <form method="post"
action="telesales?action=opportunityCreateDo&accountId=<%=
request.getParameter("accountId") %>">
```

```html
<input type="hidden" name="accountId" value="{{accountId}}">
<table border="0" cellspacing="1" cellpadding="5" bgcolor="#CCCCCC">
      <tr bgcolor="#407BA8">
            <td style="color: #ffffff; font-weight:
bold;">Account</td>
            <td bgcolor="#ffffff"><%= accountName %></td>
      </tr>
      <tr bgcolor="#407BA8">
            <td style="color: #ffffff; font-weight: bold;">Name</td>
            <td bgcolor="#ffffff"><input type="input" name="name"
style="width:250px"></td>
      </tr>
      <tr bgcolor="#407BA8">
            <td style="color: #ffffff; font-weight:
bold;">Amount</td>
            <td bgcolor="#ffffff"><input type="input" name="amount"
value="125.25"></td>
      </tr>
      <tr bgcolor="#407BA8">
            <td style="color: #ffffff; font-weight:
bold;">Stage</td>
            <td bgcolor="#ffffff">
            <select name="stageName">
                  <option>Prospecting</option>
                  <option>Qualifications</option>
                  <option>Value Proposition</option>
            </select>
            </td>
      </tr>
      <tr bgcolor="#407BA8">
            <td style="color: #ffffff; font-weight:
bold;">Probability</td>
            <td bgcolor="#ffffff">
            <select name="probability">
                  <option value="10">10%</option>
                  <option value="25">25%</option>
                  <option value="50">50%</option>
                  <option value="75">75%</option>
            </select>
            </td>
      </tr>
      <tr bgcolor="#407BA8">
```

```
                        <td style="color: #ffffff; font-weight: bold;">Close
Date</td>
                        <td bgcolor="#ffffff"><input type="input"
name="closeDate" value="1/1/2012"></td>
              </tr>
              <tr bgcolor="#407BA8">
                        <td style="color: #ffffff; font-weight:
bold;">Order</td>
                        <td bgcolor="#ffffff"><input type="input"
name="orderNumber" value="7"></td>
              </tr>
              <tr>
                        <td colspan="2" bgcolor="#ffffff" align="center"><input
type="submit" value="Submit"></td>
              </tr>
      </table>
      </form>

      There is no form validation so please fill in all fields.

</body>
</html>
```

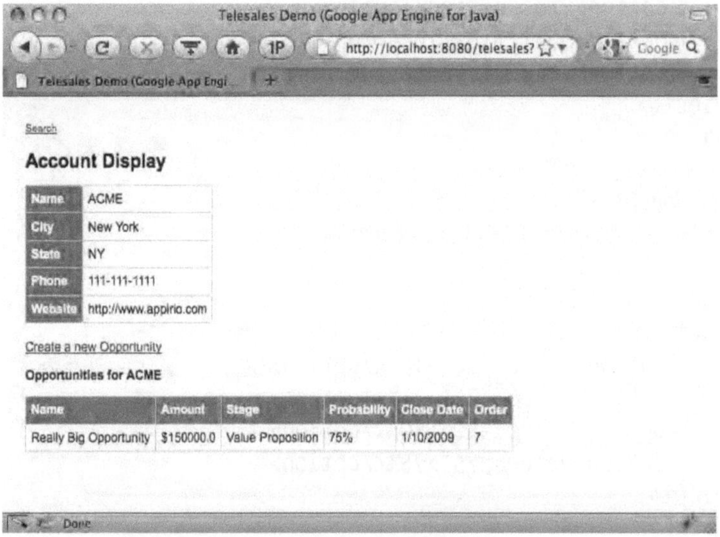

Figure 4-6. *The Account Display web page with the newly created opportunity*

Model

Our model consists of two POJOs for the Account and Opportunity objects used by the application. These domain-specific objects are constructed by the servlet and passed to and from the controller to the views. Your application uses JDO, therefore Listings 4-6 and 4-7 represent the objects along with the required annotations for JDO.

Listing 4-6. *The code for Account.java*

```java
package com.appirio.entity;

import javax.jdo.annotations.IdGeneratorStrategy;
import javax.jdo.annotations.IdentityType;
import javax.jdo.annotations.PersistenceCapable;
import javax.jdo.annotations.Persistent;
import javax.jdo.annotations.PrimaryKey;

@PersistenceCapable(identityType = IdentityType.APPLICATION)
public class Account {

    @PrimaryKey
    @Persistent(valueStrategy = IdGeneratorStrategy.IDENTITY) private Long
id;
    @Persistent private String name;
    @Persistent private String city;
    @Persistent private String state;
    @Persistent private String phone;
    @Persistent String website;

        public Account(String name, String city, String state, String phone,
String website) {
            this.name = name;
            this.city = city;
            this.state = state;
            this.phone = phone;
            this.website = website;
        }

        /**
         * @return the id
         */
        public Long getId() {
```

```java
        return id;
    }
    /**
     * @param id the id to set
     */
    public void setId(Long id) {
        this.id = id;
    }
    /**
     * @return the name
     */
    public String getName() {
        return name;
    }
    /**
     * @param name the name to set
     */
    public void setName(String name) {
        this.name = name;
    }
    /**
     * @return the city
     */
    public String getCity() {
        return city;
    }
    /**
     * @param city the city to set
     */
    public void setCity(String city) {
        this.city = city;
    }
    /**
     * @return the state
     */
    public String getState() {
        return state;
    }
    /**
     * @param state the state to set
     */
    public void setState(String state) {
```

```
                this.state = state;
        }
        /**
         * @return the phone
         */
        public String getPhone() {
                return phone;
        }
        /**
         * @param phone the phone to set
         */
        public void setPhone(String phone) {
                this.phone = phone;
        }
        /**
         * @return the website
         */
        public String getWebsite() {
                return website;
        }
        /**
         * @param website the website to set
         */
        public void setWebsite(String website) {
                this.website = website;
        }
}
```

Listing 4-7. The code for Opportunity.java

```
package com.appirio.entity;

import java.util.Date;

import javax.jdo.annotations.IdGeneratorStrategy;
import javax.jdo.annotations.IdentityType;
import javax.jdo.annotations.PersistenceCapable;
import javax.jdo.annotations.Persistent;
import javax.jdo.annotations.PrimaryKey;

@PersistenceCapable(identityType = IdentityType.APPLICATION)
public class Opportunity {
```

```java
@PrimaryKey
@Persistent(valueStrategy = IdGeneratorStrategy.IDENTITY) Long id;
@Persistent private String name;
@Persistent private double amount;
@Persistent private String stageName;
@Persistent private int probability;
@Persistent private Date closeDate;
@Persistent private int orderNumber;
@Persistent private Long accountId;

public Opportunity(String name, double amount, String stageName, int
probability, Date closeDate, int orderNumber, Long accountId) {
    this.name = name;
    this.amount = amount;
    this.stageName = stageName;
    this.probability = probability;
    this.closeDate = closeDate;
    this.orderNumber = orderNumber;
    this.accountId = accountId;
}

    /**
     * @return the id
     */
    public Long getId() {
        return id;
    }
    /**
     * @param id the id to set
     */
    public void setId(Long id) {
        this.id = id;
    }
    /**
     * @return the name
     */
    public String getName() {
        return name;
    }
    /**
     * @param name the name to set
     */
    public void setName(String name) {
```

```java
        this.name = name;
}
/**
 * @return the amount
 */
public double getAmount() {
        return amount;
}
/**
 * @param amount the amount to set
 */
public void setAmount(double amount) {
        this.amount = amount;
}
/**
 * @return the stageName
 */
public String getStageName() {
        return stageName;
}
/**
 * @param stageName the stageName to set
 */
public void setStageName(String stageName) {
        this.stageName = stageName;
}
/**
 * @return the probability
 */
public int getProbability() {
        return probability;
}
/**
 * @param probability the probability to set
 */
public void setProbability(int probability) {
        this.probability = probability;
}
/**
 * @return the closeDate
 */
public Date getCloseDate() {
```

```java
            return closeDate;
    }
    /**
     * @param closeDate the closeDate to set
     */
    public void setCloseDate(Date closeDate) {
        this.closeDate = closeDate;
    }
    /**
     * @return the orderNumber
     */
    public int getOrderNumber() {
        return orderNumber;
    }
    /**
     * @param orderNumber the orderNumber to set
     */
    public void setOrderNumber(int orderNumber) {
        this.orderNumber = orderNumber;
    }
    /**
     * @return the accountId
     */
    public Long getAccountId() {
        return accountId;
    }
    /**
     * @param accountId the accountId to set
     */
    public void setAccountId(Long accountId) {
        this.accountId = accountId;
    }
}
```

Controller

The controller processes and responds to application events and, for our
application, is implemented by a single servlet. All of the methods called from your
views are implemented in this servlet (Listing 4-8). The servlet uses an instance of
the PersistenceManager and well as some JDO Query Language (JDOQL) queries,
which we'll explain in detail in Chapter 7.

Listing 4-8. The code for TelesalesServlet.java

```java
package com.appirio;

import java.io.IOException;
import javax.servlet.http.*;

import java.util.Date;
import java.util.List;
import java.text.DateFormat;
import javax.servlet.*;
import javax.jdo.PersistenceManager;
import com.appirio.entity.*;

import com.google.appengine.api.datastore.Key;
import com.google.appengine.api.datastore.KeyFactory;

@SuppressWarnings("serial")
public class TelesalesServlet extends HttpServlet {

    public void doGet(HttpServletRequest request, HttpServletResponse
response)
                throws ServletException, IOException {

        // create the persistence manager instance
        PersistenceManager pm = PMF.get().getPersistenceManager();

        // display the lookup form
        if(request.getParameter("action").equals("accountLookup")) {

            // query for the entities by name
            String query = "select from " + Account.class.getName()
+ " where name == '"+request.getParameter("accountName")+"'";
                List<Account> accounts = (List<Account>)
pm.newQuery(query).execute();

                // pass the list to the jsp
            request.setAttribute("accounts", accounts);
            // forward the request to the jsp
            RequestDispatcher dispatcher =
getServletContext().getRequestDispatcher("/accountLookup.jsp");
            dispatcher.forward(request, response);
```

```
            // display the create new account form
          } else
if(request.getParameter("action").equals("accountCreate")) {
                    response.sendRedirect("/accountCreate.jsp");

        // process the new account creation and send the user to the
account display page
          } else
if(request.getParameter("action").equals("accountCreateDo")) {

            // create the new account
            Account a = new Account(
                request.getParameter("name"),
                request.getParameter("billingCity"),
                request.getParameter("billingState"),
                request.getParameter("phone"),
                request.getParameter("website")
            );

            // persist the entity
          try {
            pm.makePersistent(a);
          } finally {
            pm.close();
          }


response.sendRedirect("telesales?action=accountDisplay&accountId="+a.getId(
));

            // display the account details and opportunities
          } else
if(request.getParameter("action").equals("accountDisplay")) {

            // fetch the account
            Key k =
KeyFactory.createKey(Account.class.getSimpleName(), new
Integer(request.getParameter("accountId")).intValue());
            Account a = pm.getObjectById(Account.class, k);

            // query for the opportunities
```

```java
                String query = "select from " +
Opportunity.class.getName() + " where accountId ==
"+request.getParameter("accountId");
                List<Opportunity> opportunities = (List<Opportunity>)
pm.newQuery(query).execute();

                        // pass the list to the jsp
                request.setAttribute("account", a);
                        // pass the list to the jsp
                request.setAttribute("opportunities", opportunities);

                // forward the request to the jsp
                RequestDispatcher dispatcher =
getServletContext().getRequestDispatcher("/accountDisplay.jsp");
                dispatcher.forward(request, response);

            // display the create new opportunity form
            } else
if(request.getParameter("action").equals("opportunityCreate")) {

                Key k =
KeyFactory.createKey(Account.class.getSimpleName(), new
Integer(request.getParameter("accountId")).intValue());
                Account a = pm.getObjectById(Account.class, k);

                // pass the account name to the jsp
                request.setAttribute("accountName", a.getName());
                // forward the request to the jsp
                RequestDispatcher dispatcher =
getServletContext().getRequestDispatcher("/opportunityCreate.jsp");
                dispatcher.forward(request, response);

        // process the new opportunity creation and send the user to
the account display page
            } else
if(request.getParameter("action").equals("opportunityCreateDo")) {

                Date closeDate = new Date();

                // try to parse the date
            try {
            DateFormat df = DateFormat.getDateInstance(3);
```

```
                closeDate = df.parse(request.getParameter("closeDate"));
            } catch(java.text.ParseException pe) {
                System.out.println("Exception " + pe);
            }

                            // create the new opportunity
                    Opportunity opp = new Opportunity(
                        request.getParameter("name"),
                        new
Double(request.getParameter("amount")).doubleValue(),
                        request.getParameter("stageName"),
                        new
Integer(request.getParameter("probability")).intValue(),
                        closeDate,
                        new
Integer(request.getParameter("orderNumber")).intValue(),
                        new Long(request.getParameter("accountId"))
                    );

                        // persist the entity
                try {
                    pm.makePersistent(opp);
                } finally {
                    pm.close();
                }


response.sendRedirect("telesales?action=accountDisplay&accountId="+request.
getParameter("accountId"));

            }

        }

    public void doPost(HttpServletRequest request, HttpServletResponse
response)
        throws ServletException, IOException {
            doGet(request, response);
        }

    }
```

■ **Note** The servlet in Listing 4-8 describes code for interacting with Bigtable. We'll provide more details on the PersistenceManager, JDO, and JDOQL in Chapter 7.

Deployment Descriptor

When the web server receives a request for your application, it uses the deployment descriptor to map the URL of the request to the code handling the request. Modify the web.xml file with the code in Listing 4-9 to use the TelesalesServlet class. The servlet mapping specifies that all incoming requests to "telesales" be mapped to the newly created servlet defined in the servlet definition.

Listing 4-9. *The web.xml file*

```xml
<?xml version="1.0" encoding="utf-8"?>
<!DOCTYPE web-app PUBLIC
 "-//Sun Microsystems, Inc.//DTD Web Application 2.3//EN"
 "http://java.sun.com/dtd/web-app_2_3.dtd">

<web-app xmlns="http://java.sun.com/xml/ns/javaee" version="2.5">
      <servlet>
            <servlet-name>telesales</servlet-name>
            <servlet-class>com.appirio.TelesalesServlet</servlet-class>
      </servlet>
      <servlet-mapping>
            <servlet-name>telesales</servlet-name>
            <url-pattern>/telesales</url-pattern>
      </servlet-mapping>
      <welcome-file-list>
            <welcome-file>index.html</welcome-file>
      </welcome-file-list>
</web-app>
```

PersistenceManager

The servlet utilizes Bigtable to store data for your application. Listing 4-10 displays how you obtain an instance of the PersistenceManager from the PersistenceManagerFactory object. As with most datastores, obtaining a connection is expensive so you should the wrap it in a singleton.

Listing 4-10. *The code for PMF.java*

```java
package com.appirio;

import javax.jdo.JDOHelper;
import javax.jdo.PersistenceManagerFactory;

public final class PMF {

    private static final PersistenceManagerFactory pmfInstance =
        JDOHelper.getPersistenceManagerFactory("transactions-optional");
    private PMF() {}

    public static PersistenceManagerFactory get() {
        return pmfInstance;
    }

}
```

Spring MVC

Spring MVC is one of the more popular frameworks and is fully compatible with App Engine. The only modification you may have to make is if you are using Spring Forms, in which case you'll need to register custom editors for your properties.

In this section you're going to set up a quick Spring application to show the best practices and configuration to run on App Engine.

To get started, create a new Web Application Project and paste the following jar files from the Spring distribution into your /WEB-INB/lib directory. You'll also need to add the files to your build path.

- spring-web.jar

- spring-webmvc.jar

- spring-core.jar

- spring-beans.jar

- spring-context.jar

- standard.jar

- jstl.jar

- commons-logging.jar

■ **Note** Don't include the all-in-one jar (spring.jar) as it will throw java.lang.NoClassDefFoundError: javax/naming/NamingException.

Server Configuration

Modify the web.xml file generated by Eclipse with the code in Listing 4-11, to use the Spring DispatchServlet.

Listing 4-11. The web.xml file

```xml
<?xml version="1.0" encoding="utf-8"?>
<!DOCTYPE web-app PUBLIC
 "-//Sun Microsystems, Inc.//DTD Web Application 2.3//EN"
 "http://java.sun.com/dtd/web-app_2_3.dtd">

<web-app xmlns="http://java.sun.com/xml/ns/javaee" version="2.5">
    <servlet>
            <servlet-name>dispatcher</servlet-name>
            <servlet-
class>org.springframework.web.servlet.DispatcherServlet</servlet-class>
            <load-on-startup>1</load-on-startup>
    </servlet>
    <servlet-mapping>
            <servlet-name>dispatcher</servlet-name>
            <url-pattern>*.do</url-pattern>
    </servlet-mapping>
    <welcome-file-list>
            <welcome-file>index.jsp</welcome-file>
    </welcome-file-list>
</web-app>
```

Create the dispatcher-servlet.xml file in your /WEB-inf/ directory with the code from Listing 4-12. The viewResolver bean allows you to swap out rendering models without tying you to a specific view technology.

Listing 4-12. *The dispatcher-servlet.xml file*

```
<?xml version="1.0" encoding="UTF-8"?>
<beans xmlns="http://www.springframework.org/schema/beans"
       xmlns:xsi="http://www.w3.org/2001/XMLSchema-instance"
xmlns:p="http://www.springframework.org/schema/p"
       xmlns:context="http://www.springframework.org/schema/context"
       xsi:schemaLocation="http://www.springframework.org/schema/beans
http://www.springframework.org/schema/beans/spring-beans.xsd
              http://www.springframework.org/schema/context
http://www.springframework.org/schema/context/spring-context.xsd">

       <context:component-scan base-package="com.appirio" />

       <bean id="viewResolver"

       class="org.springframework.web.servlet.view.InternalResourceViewResol
ver"
              p:prefix="/WEB-INF/views/"
              p:suffix=".jsp" />

</beans>
```

Views

Now create the views for the application. First, you need a simple form that allows the user to enter a name (Figure 4-7). Listing 4-13 is the JSP page that is loaded from the deployment descriptor as the default web page. It includes a standard HTML form with a single input field.

Listing 4-13. *The index.jsp page*

```
<?xml version="1.0" encoding="ISO-8859-1" ?>
<%@ page language="java" contentType="text/html; charset=ISO-8859-1"
pageEncoding="ISO-8859-1"%>
<!DOCTYPE html PUBLIC "-//W3C//DTD XHTML 1.0 Transitional//EN"
"http://www.w3.org/TR/xhtml1/DTD/xhtml1-transitional.dtd">
<html xmlns="http://www.w3.org/1999/xhtml">
<head>
<meta http-equiv="Content-Type" content="text/html; charset=ISO-8859-1" />
<title>Spring - GAE</title>
</head>
```

```
<body>
        <form action="test.do" method="post">What's your first name? <br />
        <input type="text" name="name" /> <br />
        <input type="submit" value="Submit" /></form>
</body>
</html>
```

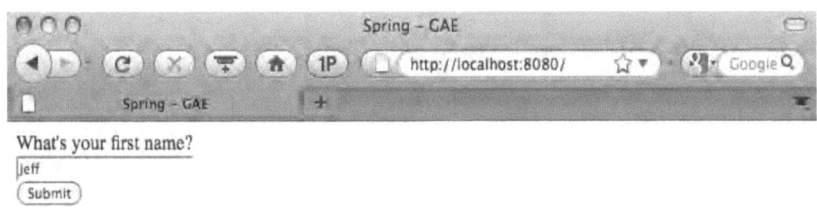

Figure 4-7. *The index.jsp page providing user input*

Now you need to create the JSP page that displays the value submitted by the user. The code in Listing 4-14 uses the JavaServer Pages Standard Tag Library to display the name that the user entered in the previous page (Figure 4-8).

Listing 4-14. *The test.jsp page*

```
<?xml version="1.0" encoding="ISO-8859-1" ?>
<%@ page language="java" contentType="text/html; charset=ISO-8859-1"
pageEncoding="ISO-8859-1"%>
<%@ page isELIgnored="false"%>
<%@taglib prefix="c" uri="http://java.sun.com/jsp/jstl/core"%>

<!DOCTYPE html PUBLIC "-//W3C//DTD XHTML 1.0 Transitional//EN"
"http://www.w3.org/TR/xhtml1/DTD/xhtml1-transitional.dtd">
<html xmlns="http://www.w3.org/1999/xhtml">
<head>
```

73

```
<meta http-equiv="Content-Type" content="text/html; charset=ISO-8859-1" />
<title>Insert title here</title>
</head>
<body>
        Hello <c:out value="${name}" />!!
</body>
</html>
```

Hello Jeff!!

Figure 4-8. *The test.jsp page displaying the standard "hello" with the user's input*

Adobe Flex

Adobe Flex is becoming a popular choice for generating the client side of enterprise Java applications. Flex applications run on the ubiquitous Adobe Flash Player and are developed using both ActionScript and MXML. MXML is a declarative, XML-based language that is preprocessed into ActionScript during compilation. You use it to create and interact with components such as panels, input fields, and data grids. ActionScript 3.0 is a powerful, object-oriented programming language that is used for the core logic of Flex applications. Flex development has a fairly low learning curve due to the striking similarity between Java and ActionScript in language features, concepts, and syntax. The languages use similar conditional statements, looping syntax, and even coding conventions (Figure 4-9).

The UI portion of Flex applications are typically constructed using MXML. This is a declarative, XML-based language that is pre-processed into ActionScript during compilation. You use MXML to create and interact with components such as panels, input fields, and data grids. We are simply providing a cursory overview of ActionScript and MXML as your application focuses more on the Java aspects of the application.

```
1   package mypackage
2   {
3       import some.pkg.*;
4
5       public class MyClass
6           extends MyParentClass
7           implements IParent
8       {
9
10          public var obj:Object = new Object();
11          private var foo:String = "foo";
12          public static const MYSTATIC:int = 10;
13
14          public function doSomething(s:String) {
15              var a:float = 10;
16              var b:String = s;
17
18              for (var i:int =  0; i<10; ++i) {
19                  // perform some actions
20              }
21
22              try {
23                  var g:int = a as int;
24              } catch (var e:Error) {
25                  throw new Error("OOPS");
26              }
27
28              return true;
29          }
30
31      }
32
33  }
```

```
1   package mypackage
2
3       import some.pkg.*;
4
5       public class MyClass
6           extends MyPrentClass
7           implements IParent
8
9       {
10
11          public Object obj = new Object();
12          private String foo = "foo";
13          public static final int MYSTATIC = 10;
14
15          public doSomething(String s) {
16              float a = 10;
17              String b = s;
18
19              for (int i = 0; i<10; ++i) {
20                  // perform some actions
21              }
22
23              try {
24                  int g = (int)f;
25              } catch (Exception e) {
26                  throw new MyException("OOPS");
27              }
28
29              return true;
30          }|
31
32      }
```

Figure 4-9. Similar classes in both ActionScript and Java

Flex communicates with Java application servers using HTTP, SOAP-based web services, or Action Message Format (AMF),), Adobe's proprietary format. You can choose from a few open-source AMF implementations including WebORB, GraniteDS, and Adobe's BlazeDS. All of these implementations provide the ability to communicate via JMS or Flex remoting. Remoting is much quicker and more efficient than using XML across the wire and is the protocol that you will be using for your application.

You are going to set up a Flex application that fetches accounts from Bigtable using GraniteDS. The remoting service is a high-performance data transfer service that allows your Flex application to directly invoke Java object methods on your application and consume the return values natively. The objects returned from the server-side methods are automatically deserialized into either dynamic or typed ActionScript objects.

If you don't already have the Flex Builder installed, you can download a 60-day trial of either the Adobe Flex Builder 3 or the Flex Builder 3 plug-in from http://www.adobe.com/cfusion/entitlement/index.cfm?e=flex3email. The plug-in may get you up and running a little quicker and it's a pretty straightforward install if you are comfortable with the Eclipse installation process.

Now create a new Web Application Project and uncheck "Use Google Web Toolkit". Since you are going to be using Flex as the front end for your application, you'll want to add the Flex Project Nature to your project. Right-click the project name in the left panel and select Flex Project Nature ➤ Add Flex Project Nature. Choose "Other" as the application server, click Next, and then click Finish. This will automatically create your Flex main.mxml file in the src directory. Once the main.mxml file has been created, the Eclipse Problems tab should display the following error message, "Cannot create HTML wrapper. Right-click here to recreate folder html-template." To fix this error, simply right-click the error message and select "Recreate HTML Templates."

Now you need to install the required jar files for GraniteDS. Download the latest version of GraniteDS from http://sourceforge.net/projects/granite/files, unzip the files, find granite.jar in the `graniteds/build/` directory, and place the jar file into your project's `/WEB-INF/lib/` directory. You'll also need to get the latest version of Xalan-J from http://www.apache.org/dyn/closer.cgi/xml/xalan-j. Unzip the files and copy serializer.jar and xalan.jar into your project's `/WEB-INF/lib/` directory.

Server Configuration

Now that you have the Flex Builder (or plug-in) set up correctly and your project created with all of its requirements, you can start configuring your application. First, you need to tell App Engine which classes GraniteDS uses as well as define its servlet mappings. Place the code shown in Listing 4-15 in the web-xml file between the `<web-app>` tags.

Listing 4-15. *The web.xml file*

```
<!-- GraniteDS -->
<listener>
    <listener-class>org.granite.config.GraniteConfigListener</listener-
class>
</listener>

<!-- handle AMF requests serialization and deserialization -->
```

```
<filter>
    <filter-name>AMFMessageFilter</filter-name>
    <filter-class>org.granite.messaging.webapp.AMFMessageFilter</filter-
class>
</filter>
<filter-mapping>
    <filter-name>AMFMessageFilter</filter-name>
    <url-pattern>/graniteamf/*</url-pattern>
</filter-mapping>

<!-- processes AMF requests -->
<servlet>
    <servlet-name>AMFMessageServlet</servlet-name>
    <servlet-
class>org.granite.messaging.webapp.AMFMessageServlet</servlet-class>
    <load-on-startup>1</load-on-startup>
</servlet>
<servlet-mapping>
    <servlet-name>AMFMessageServlet</servlet-name>
    <url-pattern>/graniteamf/*</url-pattern>
</servlet-mapping>
```

GraniteDS communicates with the servlet container through a remoting destination, which exposes a Java class to your Flex application so that it can invoke methods remotely. In Listing 4-16, the destination ID is a logical name that your Flex application uses to refer to the remote class. This eliminates the need to hard-code a reference to the fully qualified Java class name. This logical name is mapped to the Java class as part of the destination configuration in services-config.xml. Create a new folder under /WEB-INF/ called "flex" and create the services-config.xml file with the code in Listing 4-16.

Listing 4-16. *The services-config file for your remoting destination*

```
<?xml version="1.0" encoding="UTF-8"?>
<services-config>
    <services>
        <service
            id="granite-service"
            class="flex.messaging.services.RemotingService"
            messageTypes="flex.messaging.messages.RemotingMessage">
            <destination id="Gateway">
                <channels>
                    <channel ref="my-graniteamf"/>
```

```
                </channels>
                <properties>
                    <scope>application</scope>
                    <source>com.appirio.Gateway</source>
                </properties>
            </destination>
        </service>
    </services>

    <channels>
        <channel-definition id="my-graniteamf"
class="mx.messaging.channels.AMFChannel">
            <endpoint
                uri="/graniteamf/amf"
                class="flex.messaging.endpoints.AMFEndpoint"/>
        </channel-definition>
    </channels>
</services-config>
```

For Flex remoting to work correctly you need to pass some arguments to the compiler, telling it where to find the services file that defines your remoting destination. Your remoting destination points to a class called Gateway that you will create shortly. Right-click the project name in the left panel and select Properties ➤ Flex Compiler. Replace your compiler arguments with the following:

```
-locale en_US -services ../war/WEB-INF/flex/services-config.xml
```

Since you are using GraniteDS, you have to provide the runtime configuration for the container. Create a new folder called "granite" under /WEB-INF/ and paste the granite-config.xml file from graniteds/examples/graniteds_pojo/resources/WEB-INF/granite/ into it.

In this example you'll be using the Java Persistence API (JPA) as the persistence protocol. Since App Engine utilizes JDO by default, you'll need to create the configuration file for JPA manually. Create the persistence.xml file with the code from Listing 4-17 in the /src/META-INF/ directory.

Listing 4-17. *JPA persistence.xml file*

```
<?xml version="1.0" encoding="UTF-8" ?>
<persistence xmlns="http://java.sun.com/xml/ns/persistence"
    xmlns:xsi="http://www.w3.org/2001/XMLSchema-instance"
    xsi:schemaLocation="http://java.sun.com/xml/ns/persistence
```

```
          http://java.sun.com/xml/ns/persistence/persistence_1_0.xsd"
version="1.0">
    <persistence-unit name="transactions-optional">

<provider>org.datanucleus.store.appengine.jpa.DatastorePersistenceProvider<
/provider>
        <properties>
            <property name="datanucleus.NontransactionalRead"
value="true"/>
            <property name="datanucleus.NontransactionalWrite"
value="true"/>
            <property name="datanucleus.ConnectionURL"
value="appengine"/>
        </properties>
    </persistence-unit>
</persistence>
```

Client-Side Code

Designing your Flex client is much easier than you might expect. Your client will be very basic and will expose two functions through a tabbed interface. Users will be able to either create a new account or look up the details of an existing one by its ID (Figure 4-10).

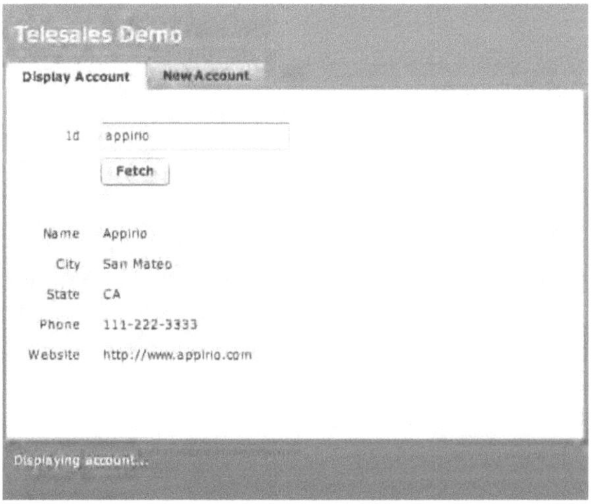

Figure 4-10. *The Flex UI displaying an account lookup*

Your Flex client will consist of a single MXML file containing all of your code and UI elements. For larger, more complex applications where you have clearly defined layers, you would typically break up the application into multiple MXML files and ActionScript classes using an MVC paradigm. Since your application is relatively small, there is really no need for this type of separation.

As you look at the code for main.mxml in Listing 4-18, pay particular attention to the RemoteObject tag at the top of the file. The ID of the tag (gateway) is used to reference the RemoteObject throughout the file, while the destination (Gateway) is the same destination you set up in your services-config.xml file specifying your remoting destination of com.appirio.Gateway.

The individual methods specified by the RemoteObject tag map directly to the public methods in the Gateway class that you will define in Listing 4-18.

Listing 4-18. *The Flex UI: main.mxml*

```
<?xml version="1.0" encoding="utf-8"?>
<mx:Application xmlns:mx="http://www.adobe.com/2006/mxml" layout="absolute"
width="500" height="400">
    <mx:RemoteObject id="gateway" destination="Gateway"
fault="status.text=event.fault.toString();">
        <mx:method name="createAccount"
result="status.text='Created.';"/>
        <mx:method name="fetchAccount" result="displayAccount(event);"/>
    </mx:RemoteObject>

    <mx:Script>
    <![CDATA[
            import mx.rpc.events.ResultEvent;

            // create the account in App Engine
            private function createAccount():void {
                // submit the create request to App Engine

        gateway.createAccount(frmId.text,frmName.text,frmCity.text,frmState.t
ext,frmPhone.text,frmWebsite.text);
                // remove current text
                status.text=null;
                frmId.text=null;
                frmName.text=null;
                frmCity.text=null;
                frmState.text=null;
```

```
                frmPhone.text=null;
                frmWebsite.text=null;
        }

        // fetch the account
        private function fetchAccount():void {
                status.text='Fetching account...';
                // fetch the account by Id from App Engine
                gateway.fetchAccount(fetchId.text);
        }

        // display the results from App Engine returned from
fetchAccount()
        private function displayAccount(event:ResultEvent):void {
                status.text='Displaying account...';
                var account:Account = event.result as Account;
                txtName.text=account.name;
                txtCity.text=account.city;
                txtState.text=account.state;
                txtPhone.text=account.phone;
                txtWebsite.text=account.website;
        }

    ]]>
    </mx:Script>

  <mx:Text x="10" y="14" text="Telesales Demo" fontSize="18"
color="#FFFFFF"/>
      <mx:TabNavigator left="5" right="5" bottom="50" top="50">
            <mx:Canvas label="Display Account" width="100%" height="100%">
                  <mx:Form width="100%" height="100%" left="0">
                        <mx:FormItem label="Id">
                              <mx:TextInput id="fetchId"/>
                        </mx:FormItem>
                        <mx:FormItem>
                              <mx:Button label="Fetch"
click="fetchAccount();"/>
                        </mx:FormItem>
                        <mx:FormItem>
                              <mx:Spacer/>
                        </mx:FormItem>
```

```
                            <mx:FormItem label="Name">
                                    <mx:Text id="txtName"/>
                            </mx:FormItem>
                            <mx:FormItem label="City">
                                    <mx:Text id="txtCity"/>
                            </mx:FormItem>
                            <mx:FormItem label="State">
                                    <mx:Text id="txtState"/>
                            </mx:FormItem>
                            <mx:FormItem label="Phone">
                                    <mx:Text id="txtPhone"/>
                            </mx:FormItem>
                            <mx:FormItem label="Website">
                                    <mx:Text id="txtWebsite"/>
                            </mx:FormItem>
                    </mx:Form>
            </mx:Canvas>
            <mx:Canvas label="New Account" width="100%" height="100%">
                    <mx:Form width="100%" height="100%" left="0">
                            <mx:FormItem label="Id">
                                    <mx:TextInput id="frmId"/>
                            </mx:FormItem>
                            <mx:FormItem label="Name">
                                    <mx:TextInput id="frmName"/>
                            </mx:FormItem>
                            <mx:FormItem label="City">
                                    <mx:TextInput id="frmCity"/>
                            </mx:FormItem>
                            <mx:FormItem label="State">
                                    <mx:TextInput id="frmState"/>
                            </mx:FormItem>
                            <mx:FormItem label="Phone">
                                    <mx:TextInput id="frmPhone"/>
                            </mx:FormItem>
                            <mx:FormItem label="Website">
                                    <mx:TextInput id="frmWebsite"/>
                            </mx:FormItem>
                            <mx:FormItem>
                                    <mx:Button label="Save"
    click="createAccount()"/>
                            </mx:FormItem>
```

```
                </mx:Form>
            </mx:Canvas>
        </mx:TabNavigator>
        <mx:Text x="10" y="358" id="status" color="#FFFFFF" width="200"/>
```

```
</mx:Application>
```

Now you need to create an Account value object to hold the data returned from the server. Right-click the src folder and select New ➤ ActionScript Class. Enter the class name "Account" and click Finish. Add the code in Listing 4-19 to this class. Notice that the code uses the [RemoteClass(alias=" com.appirio.Account")] annotation to map the ActionScript version of the Account class (Account.as) to the Java version (Account.java). As a result, Account objects returned by the fetchAccount() method of the service layer are deserialized into instances of the ActionScript Account class automatically.

Listing 4-19. *The Account.as file*

```
package
{
    [Bindable]
    [RemoteClass(alias="com.appirio.Account")]
    public class Account
    {

        public var id:String;
        public var name:String;
        public var city:String;
        public var state:String;
        public var phone:String;
        public var website:String;


    }
}
```

Server-Side Code

Your client-side code is now complete and you can jump back to the server side to finish up your application. You need to add the JPA entity that will store your data in App Engine. Create the Account class with the code from Listing 4-20. This class will consist of the same members as the ActionScript class so that GraniteDS can translate them back and forth for you. We won't go into the specifics of JPA as we will cover this topic in more detail in Chapter 7.

Listing 4-20. *The Account entity class*

```
package com.appirio;

import javax.persistence.Entity;
import javax.persistence.Id;

@Entity public class Account {
        @Id String id;
        String name;
        String city;
        String state;
        String phone;
        String website;

        public Account(String id, String name, String city, String state,
String phone, String website) {
                this.id = id;
                this.name = name;
                this.city = city;
                this.state = state;
                this.phone = phone;
                this.website = website;
        }

        /**
         * @return the id
         */
        public String getId() {
                return id;
        }
        /**
         * @return the name
         */
        public String getName() {
                return name;
        }
        /**
         * @param name the name to set
```

```java
     */
    public void setName(String name) {
        this.name = name;
    }
    /**
     * @return the city
     */
    public String getCity() {
        return city;
    }
    /**
     * @param city the city to set
     */
    public void setCity(String city) {
        this.city = city;
    }
    /**
     * @return the state
     */
    public String getState() {
        return state;
    }
    /**
     * @param state the state to set
     */
    public void setState(String state) {
        this.state = state;
    }
    /**
     * @return the phone
     */
    public String getPhone() {
        return phone;
    }
    /**
     * @param phone the phone to set
     */
    public void setPhone(String phone) {
        this.phone = phone;
    }
    /**
     * @return the website
```

```
    */
    public String getWebsite() {
        return website;
    }
    /**
     * @param website the website to set
     */
    public void setWebsite(String website) {
        this.website = website;
    }
}
```

Like any datastore, you need to create a connection to fetch data. To obtain a connection to Bigtable you need to obtain an instance of the EntityManagerFactory. The implementation is pretty straightforward, but like your JDO example, you want to wrap this into a singleton due to the high connection overhead. Use the code in Listing 4-21 to create the EMF class.

Listing 4-21. *The EMF singleton*

```
package com.appirio;

import javax.persistence.EntityManagerFactory;
import javax.persistence.Persistence;

public class EMF {
    private static final EntityManagerFactory emf =
Persistence.createEntityManagerFactory("transactions-optional");

    public static EntityManagerFactory get() {
        return emf;
    }

    private EMF() {
    }
}
```

The last bit of code you need to write for your application will implement the Gateway class that GraniteDS uses as the remoting endpoint. The Gateway object in Listing 4-22 contains the public methods that the Flex front end calls via the RemoteObject tag in main.mxml. Notice that you are not doing any special type of casting for the Flex front end as GraniteDS takes care of that for you.

Listing 4-22. *The Gateway service object*

```java
package com.appirio;

import javax.persistence.EntityManager;
import javax.persistence.EntityTransaction;

public class Gateway {

    public void createAccount(String id, String name, String city, String
state, String phone, String website) {

        EntityManager em = EMF.get().createEntityManager();
        EntityTransaction tx = em.getTransaction();

        Account account = new Account(id, name, city, state, phone,
website);

        try {
            tx.begin();
            em.persist(account);
            tx.commit();
        } finally {
            if (tx.isActive()) {
                tx.rollback();
            }
            em.close();
        }

    }

    public Account fetchAccount(String id) {

        EntityManager em = EMF.get().createEntityManager();
        return em.find(Account.class, id);

    }

}
```

Running the application should now result in an application that looks like Figure 4-10. When you deploy this application to App Engine, it will also deploy the required supporting Flex files for you.

Summary

Many popular Java libraries and frameworks run on App Engine. Google doesn't officially support these projects but it does take a community-oriented approach to compatibility. There is an active and vibrant community dedicated to interoperability of these projects. While some frameworks work with minor configuration changes, others fail due to App Engine restrictions or unsupported classes.

In this chapter you built three applications using various technologies and frameworks. Out of the box App Engine uses servlets and JSPs for web applications. You built a small telesales application that used JSPs for the views, simple POJOs for the model, and a single servlet for the controller. The application used Bigtable to store and retrieve data with the JDO API.

You also created an application using the Spring MVC framework. The application was light on actual functionality but was developed to show the best practices and configuration needed to run on App Engine.

Your last application was developed using Adobe Flex for the front-end and using GraniteDS for the remoting protocol. Remoting is much quicker and more efficient than using XML across the wire and allows Flex applications to directly invoke remote Java object methods and consume the return values natively. We walked through the client-side MXML and ActionScript code development as well as the server-side. We also took an in depth look at the server configuration to provide interoperability with remoting.

In our next chapter you'll actually start building your demo application. We'll explore the functional as well as technical requirements and start developing the front-end using Google Web Toolkit.

CHAPTER 5

■ ■ ■

Developing Your Application

In the last chapter we looked at some of the libraries and frameworks that are compatible with App Engine plus some sample applications that run on App Engine's servlet container. Now it's time to roll up your sleeves and get to work. To make your application a little more interesting, you are going to be writing the presentation layer using Google Web Toolkit (GWT).). We'll examine the functional and technical specifications for the project and then walk through the code over the next couple of chapters.

If you are reading this book, you are probably a software engineer. At some time or another you have probably worked as a consultant writing code for clients for money, billing your work as a fixed-price job or as time and expense. If you've done any time-and-expense work, then you are familiar with reporting your time to clients and having them pay you for your efforts. If this is the case, then the application you will be building will be quite familiar to you.

Functional Specifications

You will be building a simple timecard-entry system throughout the next couple of chapters. Your application won't have all of the bells and whistles of a commercial-grade system, but it will have enough to really sink your teeth into Google App Engine and GWT, to a certain extent.

The basic functionality of your application should include:

- Authentication against some type of user repository to provide users with their own project settings and data.

- The ability for users to select a date range so that they can enter time for any start day of the week.

- A picklist for displaying a list of all projects that users are working on so that they can report time against each project.

- A picklist with project-specific milestones that users can report time against.

- An indicator for reporting whether the entry is billable or non-billable.

- Input fields allowing users to enter time for individual days of the week, from Monday to Sunday.

- A subtotal of hours for all entries for a particular week, organized by project and milestone.

- A grand total of all hours for the current timecard.

- The ability to click a button to add a new time-entry row to the application.

- The ability to click a Save button that persists users' entries to some type of data store and clears the user interface of all entries.

- The ability to display all of the timecard entries that a user has submitted.

- The ability for users to log out of their sessions and exit the application.

Timecard UI Mock-up

Since this is the era of Web 2.0, you should put a slick interface on the application, with dynamic page refreshes, flashy transitions, and AJAX calls. Figure 5-1 shows a mock-up what your final application should look like.

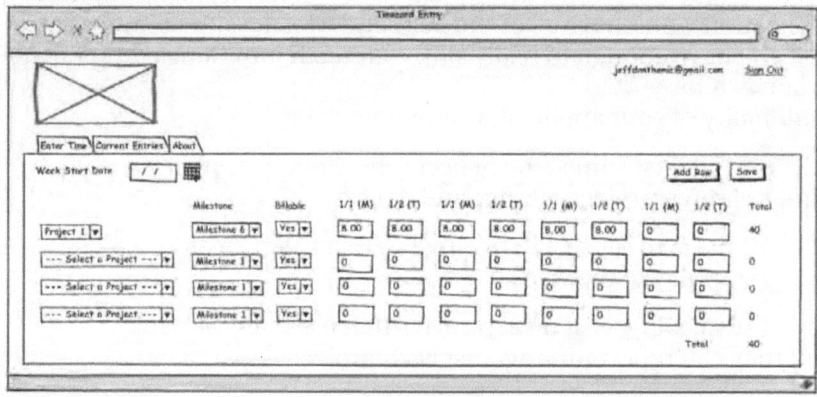

Figure 5-1. *Proposed timecard UI design*

■ **Note** I want to stress that you will not be building a production-quality application. Some features and functionality will be missing. This is due mainly to the fact that this is a beginning-level book, and we want to demonstrate just the basics and not overwhelm you with endless lines of rote code. Try not to focus too much on the functional requirements.

Technical Specifications

One of the great things about Google App Engine is that it supports so many languages, libraries, and frameworks, giving you a large number of tools with which to build your application. To implement your functional requirements you are going to use GWT and several services and technologies provided by Google and App Engine.

Authentication

Since you are using Java, you can roll your own authentication framework using the servlet session interface, App Engine's data store, and its caching service. An easier way, and the one you'll implement, is to use Google Accounts service. This service allows App Engine to authenticate your users with Google Accounts, providing for a much cleaner experience. App Engine can determine whether your application's user has logged in with their Google accounts, and can redirect them to the standard Google Accounts login page or allow them to create a new account. App Engine can also detect whether the current user is a Google Accounts administrator, making it easy to present them with content or functionality applicable to their access level. You'll use Google Accounts to set up authentication for your application in Chapter 6.

Presentation

App Engines supports a number of frameworks that should be familiar to the average Java developer. Other frameworks are either totally incompatible (for example, RichFaces) or semicompatible (for example, JBoss Seam, Wicket). As you saw in Chapter 4, the App Engine environment provides you with a Java 6 JVM, a Java servlets interface, and support for standard interfaces. This makes writing MVC web applications very straightforward if you are familiar with servlets and JavaServer Pages (JSPs).). Servlets and JSPs have their pros and cons but most seasoned developers can get an application up and running in no time.

However, since servlets and JSPs are so "Web 1.0," you are going to be developing your presentation layer using Google Web Toolkit (GWT).). If you've ever done any web development, you know how frustrating, time consuming, and error prone it is to write the sexy, dynamic applications that users crave, given the ways that different browsers and versions of browsers interpret your code. With GWT, you write your AJAX front end in Java, and GWT then compiles it into optimized JavaScript that automagically works across all major browsers. You get the "Web 2.0" functionality without all of the hassle of writing cross-compatible JavaScript on the client side.

Persistence

It's an understatement to say that virtually all applications need a way to persist their data. This could be user-generated data or simply configuration settings required by your application at runtime. Some frameworks and web application servers are distributed with lightweight, embedded databases, but App Engine comes with a massive, scalable database called Bigtable. Bigtable is a flexible, schema-less object database or entity store. It supports massive data sets with millions of entities and petabytes of data across thousands of commodity servers. Many projects at Google store data in Bigtable, including web indexing, Google Earth, and Google Finance. Using Bigtable, your applications can take advantage of the same fault-tolerant storage that Google relies on to run its business.

Your timecard application will use Bigtable to store the daily time entries that users enter. Your application will be inserting and querying for entities but not updating them. We'll be covering Bigtable and topics such as scalability, JDO, JPA, and JDOQL in more detail in Chapter 7.

Using Google Web Toolkit

As previously stated, you will be using GWT for your front end. GWT isn't a server-side framework like Spring and GraniteDS but an entirely separate product that Google has recently baked into App Engine using its Eclipse plug-in. Just as App Engine doesn't depend entirely on GWT, GWT can run just fine without App Engine. You can write GWT applications that can be embedded into HTML pages or used with other application servers. You can run a GWT application on a PHP/MySQL stack if you'd like.

One of the main advantages of GWT is that it hides the complexity of writing cross-browser JavaScript. You write your AJAX front end in Java, which GWT then cross-compiles into optimized JavaScript that automatically works across all major browsers. During development, you can iterate functionality quickly with the same methodology you're accustomed to with JavaScript, but with the Eclipse IDE you can step through and debug your Java code line by line in the same toolset that you are already comfortable with. When you're ready to deploy your application to App Engine, GWT compiles your source code into optimized, stand-alone JavaScript that works across all major browsers. GWT enables you to:

- Communicate with back-end servers using GWT RPC, JSON, and XML. With GWT RPC you can specify remote endpoints to call across the Internet with remarkable ease. GWT does the heavy lifting for you by serializing arguments, invoking the methods on the server, and deserializing the return values.

- Create UI components that can be packaged and reused in other projects.

- Develop your own JavaScript functionality to include in your applications using JavaScript Native Interface (JSNI).).

- Support for the browser Back button and history. You don't have to waste time programming the lack of state in your application.

- Use GWT-deferred binding techniques to create compact internationalized applications based on user profiles.

- Get started right away using your favorite tools like Eclipse, JUnit, and JProfiler.

■ **Note** This book is not intended to be a deep-dive into GWT but should provide just enough information to allow you to understand the technology and get you started developing with GWT. For more details on developing with GWT, check out http://tinyurl.com/o3vcpg.

Creating Your Project

Creating your project is a snap using the Google plug-in for Eclipse. Select File ➤ New ➤ Web Application Project and enter the information for your project. Ensure that you check "Use Google Web Toolkit" and "Use Google App Engine" and that you are using the latest version of each SDK. Fortunately, Eclipse will notify you when a new version of either SDK is available for download. After the wizard finishes, you will see that it has created a number of files to get your project up and running quickly (see Figure 5-2). As you work through your application, you will be replacing the code generated by the Eclipse plug-in with your own code.

```
▼ 📂 TimeEntry
   ▼ 📂 src
      ▼ 📁 com.appirio.timeentry
            📄 TimeEntry.gwt.xml
      ▼ 📁 com.appirio.timeentry.client
         ► 📄 GreetingService.java
         ► 📄 GreetingServiceAsync.java
         ► 📄 TimeEntry.java
      ▼ 📁 com.appirio.timeentry.server
         ► 📄 GreetingServiceImpl.java
      ► 📁 META-INF
         📄 log4j.properties
   ► 📦 App Engine SDK [App Engine (1) - 1.2.2]
   ► 📦 GWT SDK [GWT (1) - 1.7.0]
   ► 📦 JRE System Library [JVM 1.5.0 (MacOS X Default)]
   ▼ 📂 war
      ▼ 📂 WEB-INF
         ► 📂 lib
            📄 appengine-web.xml
            📄 logging.properties
            📄 web.xml
         📄 TimeEntry.css
         📄 TimeEntry.html
```

Figure 5-2. *Initial files and directories created by the new project wizard*

We'll be going through each of these files in detail during the development cycle, but it's important to touch on a few of the generated files that we will skim over during this process. Table 5-1 provides a summary of each file.

GWT Module Definition

In the TimeEntry.xml file, you specify your application's entry-point class, `TimeEntry.java`. In order to compile, a GWT module must specify an entry point. If a GWT module has no entry point, then it can be inherited only by other modules. You can include other modules that have entry points specified in their module XML files. If your module has multiple entry points, then each one is executed in the specified sequence.

The Host Page

For your project the code for the web application executes within the TimeEntry.html page, a.k.a the "host" page. The host page references the JavaScript source code that renders the dynamic elements of your HTML page. You can either let Eclipse dynamically generate the entire contents of the body element for you, or you can render the application in your existing web page as part of a larger application. In the latter case, you simply need to create an HTML `<div>` element to use as placeholder for the dynamically generated portions of the page.

The host page also references the application style sheet, TimeEntry.css, as well as the default GWT style sheet, standard.css, from the module definition. Eclipse generates three different themes for you, and you can choose the one you like best by uncommenting one of the lines. You'll be adding a few of your own styles to the TimeEntry.css file to give your application a nice look and feel.

Table 5-1. Project files created by the Eclipse plug-in

File	Description
TimeEntry.gwt.xml	GWT module definition. The module definition includes the collection of resources that comprise a GWT application or a shared package. By default, all applications inherit the core GWT functionality required for every project. You can also specify other GWT modules from which to inherit.
GreetingService.java	Interface for the client-side service that extends RemoteService and lists all RPC methods.
GreetingServiceAsync.java	Asynchronous service interface that is called from the client-side code.
TimeEntry.java	GWT entry point class. You'll be writing most of your code here.
GreetingServiceImpl.java	Server-side implementation of the RPC service that extends RemoteServiceServlet and implements the GreetingService interface.
appengine-web.xml	App Engine Java application configuration file specifies the application's registered application ID and the version identifier.
web.xml	Java web application descriptor containing the servlet definitions and mappings and welcome file setting.
TimeEntry.css	Application style sheet referenced by the host page.
TimeEntry.html	Host page rendering your GWT application.

Running the Initial Starter Application

Take a look at the starter application that Eclipse generated, as shown in Figure 5-3. Select the application folder on the left and choose Run ➤ Run as ➤ Web Application. This will start your application, in hosted mode, opening two windows: the hosted mode browser and the development shell. The development shell contains a log viewer displaying status and error messages while the hosted mode browser contains your initial starter application.

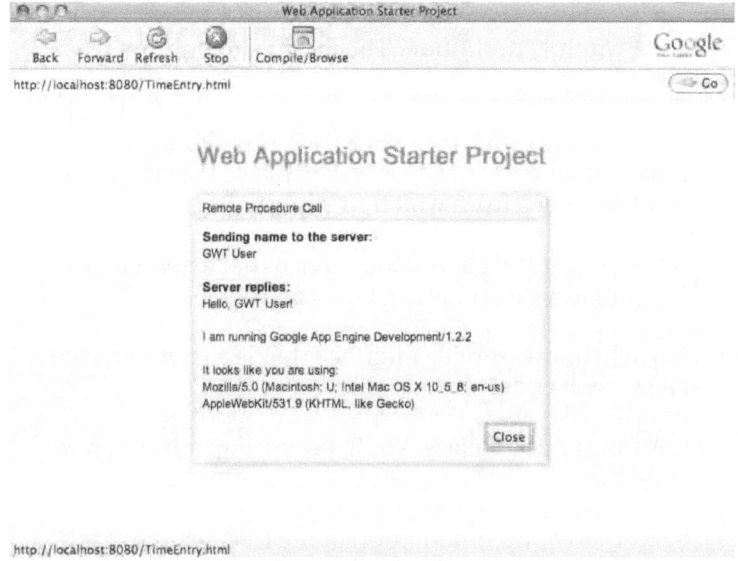

Figure 5-3. *Your starter application*

Your GWT application runs in two modes, hosted and web. The power of GWT lies in its ability to use the Eclipse IDE for front-end development.

Hosted Mode

For ease of use, GWT comes bundled with its own internal Jetty web server, but you can use your own server. The Jetty instance serves up your application directly out of the project's WAR directory. You will spend most of your development time running in hosted mode. When running in this mode your code is interacting with GWT without compiling it into JavaScript. The JVM is merely executing your application code as compiled bytecode and piping the results into the hosted mode browser.

One of the nice features of hosted mode is that you don't have to restart the hosted mode browser each time you make modifications to your source code. You can simply click the Refresh button on the hosted-mode browser, and your code is recompiled and loaded into that browser. However, if you make configuration or server-side code changes, you will need to click the Restart Server button to cycle Jetty and reload your application.

Hosted mode is the "magic" that makes GWT unique. By running your code as Java bytecode instead of JavaScript, you can take advantage of Eclipse's debugging capabilities to debug your server-side Java code *and* your client-side GWT (JavaScript) code. With GWT, gone are the days of writing debug comments to the browser window, displaying pop-ups for breakpoint messages, and, for that matter, using Firebug. With GWT and Eclipse, you can do the code-test-debug steps in one integrated environment, which dramatically increases productivity and reduces the number of runtime, client-side errors. In hosted mode you can use the Eclipse debugger to catch exceptions that normally occur in the browser, presenting users with ugly errors.

Web Mode

At some point in your development cycle you will want to start testing your application with your target browsers to check the performance and see how your application looks, feels, and operates on different browsers. Click the Compile/Browse button on the hosted mode browser toolbar and GWT will compile your source code into optimized JavaScript. You can then test your application, as it will be deployed on any browser you'd like by using the same URL as in hosted mode.

Developing Your Application

Now you'll start designing your application's UI. If you have experience developing Java applications using Swing, GWT will be an easy transition for you. Even if you've never touched Swing, you should be able to jump in and start laying out applications with a minimal learning curve.

GWT was designed for the front end and provides a rich set of UI components for implementing your design specifications. A well-defined look and feel is very important as you begin this stage. It really helps if you have a clearly defined UI, as retooling visual components down the road can become quite tedious. As you can see in Figure 5-4, you will be incorporating a variety of widgets in your application, but almost everything is built upon panels. GWT provides a wide range of panels (see Table 5-2) that can be nested in the same way that you might nest HTML tables or div elements on web pages.

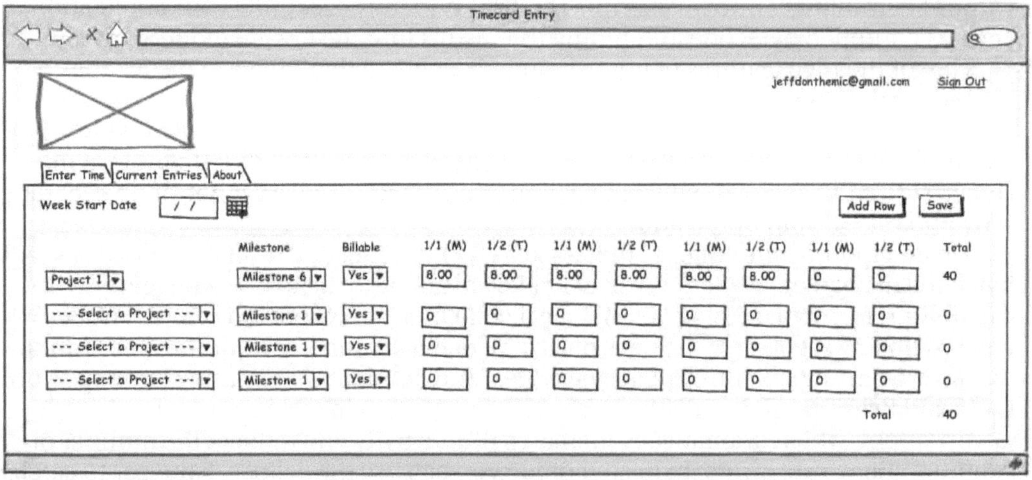

Figure 5-4. *Proposed timecard UI design displaying the major layout components*

Your application will use a `VerticalPanel` to hold all of your visual elements. The top section of the panel will consist of a `HorizontalPanel` holding your logo, email address, and sign-out link, while the bottom portion will hold a `TabPanel` with a number of interfaces.

The first tab is where your users will perform most of their work. It will consist of a `HorizontalPanel` holding a date picker, Add Row and Save buttons, and a `FlexTable` allowing users to enter their time per day. The bottom of the tab will also have a `HorizontalPanel` holding the total number of hours for the timecard.

The second tab will display the hours that the user has entered into the timecard in a `FlexTable`. It will be a simple listing and users will not be allowed to edit or delete entries.

The last panel will contain some text describing your application.

■ **Note** Some of the new features for the recently announced GWT 2.0 include an improved layout system and the UiBuilder service. This proposed service will generate widget and DOM structures from XML markup. This approach is very similar to what you see in Adobe Flex or other XML layout frameworks.

Table 5-2. Summary of GWT layout panels

Panel		Description
DisclosurePanel	▼ Click to dis This widget is is ¿ by the disclosure	A widget that consists of a header and a content panel that displays the content when a user clicks the header.
DockPanel	 north (0) west (1) · west (2) · center (5) · east (3) south (4)	A panel that arranges its child widgets "docked" at its outer edges, and allows its last widget to take up the remaining space in its center.
FlowPanel	0 · 1 · 2 3 · 4	A panel that formats its child widgets using the default HTML layout behavior.
HorizontalPanel	0 · 1 · 2	A panel that arranges its widgets in a single horizontal column.

Panel		Description
HorizontalSplitPanel		A panel that arranges two widgets in a single horizontal row and allows the user to interactively change the proportion of the width dedicated to each of the two widgets. Widgets contained within a HorizontalSplitPanel will be automatically decorated with scrollbars when necessary.
PopupPanel		A panel that can "pop up" over other widgets. It overlays the browser's client area (and any previously created pop-ups).
StackPanel		A panel that stacks its children vertically, displaying only one at a time, with a header for each child, which the user can click to display.
TabPanel		A panel that represents a tabbed set of pages, each of which contains a widget. Its child widgets are shown as the user selects the various tabs associated with them. The tabs can contain arbitrary HTML.

Panel		Description
VerticalPanel		A panel that arranges its widgets in a single vertical column.
VerticalSplitPanel		A panel that arranges two widgets in a single vertical column and allows the user to interactively change the proportion of the height dedicated to each of the two widgets. Widgets contained within a VerticalSplitterPanel will be automatically decorated with scrollbars when necessary.

Required Imports

To get started you'll need to add some imports for the GWT components that you'll be using. Open TimeEntry.java and add the following imports:

```
import com.google.gwt.core.client.EntryPoint;
import com.google.gwt.user.client.ui.Button;
import com.google.gwt.user.client.ui.FlexTable;
import com.google.gwt.user.client.ui.Label;
import com.google.gwt.user.client.ui.RootPanel;
import com.google.gwt.user.client.ui.VerticalPanel;
import com.google.gwt.user.client.ui.HorizontalPanel;
import com.google.gwt.user.client.ui.DockPanel;
import com.google.gwt.user.datepicker.client.DateBox;
import com.google.gwt.user.client.ui.AbsolutePanel;
import com.google.gwt.i18n.client.DateTimeFormat;
import com.google.gwt.user.client.ui.HasHorizontalAlignment;
import com.google.gwt.user.client.ui.Anchor;
import com.google.gwt.user.client.ui.Image;
import com.google.gwt.user.client.ui.DecoratedTabPanel;
```

```
import com.google.gwt.user.client.ui.ListBox;
import com.google.gwt.user.client.ui.TextBox;
import com.google.gwt.user.client.ui.CheckBox;
import com.google.gwt.event.dom.client.ClickEvent;
import com.google.gwt.event.dom.client.ClickHandler;
import com.google.gwt.event.logical.shared.ValueChangeEvent;
import com.google.gwt.event.logical.shared.ValueChangeHandler;
import com.google.gwt.user.client.ui.HTMLTable;
import com.google.gwt.user.client.Window;
import com.google.gwt.i18n.client.NumberFormat;
import java.util.Date;
```

Coding Your UI

Now you'll start adding your layout and UI components. We will demonstrate
different techniques for working with your components to provide examples of how
flexible GWT can be. Initialize some of your main components as private class
instance variables:

```
private VerticalPanel mainPanel = new VerticalPanel();
private AbsolutePanel totalPanel = new AbsolutePanel();
private DockPanel navPanel = new DockPanel();
private HorizontalPanel topPanel = new HorizontalPanel();
private Label totalLabel = new Label("0.00");
private FlexTable flexEntryTable = new FlexTable();
private FlexTable flexCurrentTable = new FlexTable();
private Image logo = new Image();
```

You'll eventually add sign-in functionality to your timecard, but initially your
application will be displayed as soon as your host page loads in the user's browser.
With this configuration you'll implement your code in the onModuleLoad method.

Your first line of code sets the logo for your UI. Create a folder under the
/war/ directory called "images," and drop in your favorite logo. Next, create a
HorizontalPanel, set the width to 1000px to provide enough real estate to work
with, and then add your logo, e-mail address, and sign-out link. You'll also need to
align the user information to the right to make things look nice.

```
logo.setUrl("images/appiriologo.png");

HorizontalPanel userPanel = new HorizontalPanel();
Anchor logOutLink = new Anchor("Sign Out");
Label separator = new Label("|");
```

```
separator.setStyleName("separator");
userPanel.add(new Label("jeffdonthemic@gmail.com"));
userPanel.add(separator);
userPanel.add(logOutLink);

topPanel.setWidth("1000px");
topPanel.add(logo);
topPanel.add(userPanel);
topPanel.setCellHorizontalAlignment(userPanel,
HasHorizontalAlignment.ALIGN_RIGHT);
```

Add your next HorizontalPanel to hold the date picker and the Action button. You'll also do some alignment to get the UI to look the way you want using a DockPanel.

```
// set up a horizontal panel to hold the date picker
HorizontalPanel leftNav = new HorizontalPanel();
leftNav.setSpacing(5);
leftNav.add(new Label("Week Start Date"));
DateBox dateBox = new DateBox();
dateBox.setWidth("100px");
dateBox.setFormat(new
DateBox.DefaultFormat(DateTimeFormat.getFormat("M/d/yyyy")));
leftNav.add(dateBox);

// set up a horizontal panel to hold the Add and Save buttons
HorizontalPanel buttonPanel = new HorizontalPanel();
buttonPanel.setSpacing(5);
Button addRowButton = new Button("Add Row");
Button saveButton = new Button("Save");
buttonPanel.add(addRowButton);
buttonPanel.add(saveButton);

// set up another horizontal panel to dock all of the buttons to the right
final HorizontalPanel rightNav = new HorizontalPanel();
rightNav.setHorizontalAlignment(HasHorizontalAlignment.ALIGN_RIGHT);
rightNav.setWidth("100%");
rightNav.add(buttonPanel);

// add all of the navigation panels to the dock panel
navPanel.setWidth("1000px");
navPanel.add(leftNav, DockPanel.WEST);
navPanel.add(rightNav, DockPanel.EAST);
```

Add a final HorizontalPanel to hold the grand total for the timecard that will appear at the bottom of the UI under the FlexTable.

```
// set up a horizontal panel to hold the grand total
totalPanel.setSize("1000px","50px");
totalPanel.add(new Label("Total:"), 900, 25);
totalPanel.add(totalLabel, 950, 25);
```

Now you'll start setting up your FlexPanel that will consist of the main UI component for your application. First, you set the width of the table to expand the entire width of your tabbed interface, and then you add all of your columns and headers.

```
// set the width of the table to expand the size of the navPanel
flexEntryTable.setWidth("100%");
// set the style for the table to be accessed in the css
flexEntryTable.setStylePrimaryName("timeEntryTable");

// add the columns and headers
flexEntryTable.setText(0, 0, "Project");
flexEntryTable.setText(0, 1, "Milestone");
flexEntryTable.setText(0, 2, "Billable?");
flexEntryTable.setText(0, 3, "Mon");
flexEntryTable.setText(0, 4, "Tue");
flexEntryTable.setText(0, 5, "Wed");
flexEntryTable.setText(0, 6, "Thu");
flexEntryTable.setText(0, 7, "Fri");
flexEntryTable.setText(0, 8, "Sat");
flexEntryTable.setText(0, 9, "Sun");
flexEntryTable.setText(0, 10, "Total");
```

Now you need to add all of the relevant UI components to your tabbed interface. Create a new VerticalPanel to hold the date picker, buttons, FlexTable, and grand total, and add this new panel to the first tab. Add your tabbed panel, set the width, and enable animation. Add your UI to the first tab. You'll set some properties of your tabbed interface and make sure the first tab is the one that your users see by default when your application loads. You'll be adding more tabs to your panel later on.

```
VerticalPanel tab1Content = new VerticalPanel();
tab1Content.add(navPanel);
tab1Content.add(flexEntryTable);
tab1Content.add(totalPanel);
```

```
DecoratedTabPanel tabPanel = new DecoratedTabPanel();
tabPanel.setWidth("100%");
tabPanel.setAnimationEnabled(true);
tabPanel.add(tab1Content, "Enter Time");
tabPanel.selectTab(0);
```

The last thing to do in your **onModuleLoad** method is to add all of your components to the **RootPanel**.

```
// add the navpanel and flex table to the main panel
mainPanel.add(topPanel);
mainPanel.add(tabPanel);
// associate the main panel with the HTML host page.
RootPanel.get("timeentryUI").add(mainPanel);
```

The Root panel is a special container that sits at the top of the GWT user interface hierarchy. It's an invisible container for your dynamic elements that is, by default, wrapped in a **<body>** element in your HTML host page. You'll make some changes to your generated host page to wrap the Root panel in a **<div>** element instead.

One of the major functional requirements for your application is to provide users with the ability to add new time-entry rows to the timecard. Each row will consist of a **list box** for projects, a **list box** for project-dependent milestones, **text boxes** for each day of the week, and a **label** for the row total. You'll add the following code to accomplish this task and then we'll look at how to call this method via the Add Row button click event when you implement listeners for your application. You can add a call to this method after the Root panel is set, allowing users to see a blank row when the application initially loads.

It is important to note that the two **list boxes** are defined as final, which allows your code to access the components from different methods and to fill their contents from your server-side code.

```
private void addRow() {

        int row = flexEntryTable.getRowCount();

        final ListBox lbMilestones = new ListBox(false);
        final ListBox lbProjects = new ListBox(false);
        lbProjects.addItem("-- Select a Project --");

        // create the time input fields for all 7 days
        final TextBox day1 = new TextBox();
```

```
        day1.setValue("0");
        day1.setWidth("50px");
        day1.setEnabled(false);
        final TextBox day2 = new TextBox();
        day2.setValue("0");
        day2.setWidth("50px");
        day2.setEnabled(false);
        final TextBox day3 = new TextBox();
        day3.setValue("0");
        day3.setWidth("50px");
        day3.setEnabled(false);
        final TextBox day4 = new TextBox();
        day4.setValue("0");
        day4.setWidth("50px");
        day4.setEnabled(false);
        final TextBox day5 = new TextBox();
        day5.setValue("0");
        day5.setWidth("50px");
        day5.setEnabled(false);
        final TextBox day6 = new TextBox();
        day6.setValue("0");
        day6.setWidth("50px");
        day6.setEnabled(false);
        final TextBox day7 = new TextBox();
        day7.setValue("0");
        day7.setWidth("50px");
        day7.setEnabled(false);

        // add all of the widgets to the flex table
        flexEntryTable.setWidget(row, 0, lbProjects);
        flexEntryTable.setWidget(row, 1, lbMilestones);
        flexEntryTable.setWidget(row, 2, new CheckBox());
        flexEntryTable.setWidget(row, 3, day1);
        flexEntryTable.setWidget(row, 4, day2);
        flexEntryTable.setWidget(row, 5, day3);
        flexEntryTable.setWidget(row, 6, day4);
        flexEntryTable.setWidget(row, 7, day5);
        flexEntryTable.setWidget(row, 8, day6);
        flexEntryTable.setWidget(row, 9, day7);
        flexEntryTable.setWidget(row, 10, new Label("0.00"));

    }
```

Adding Your Styles

When it comes to styling your application, GWT wisely defers to Cascading Style Sheets (CSS),), which allow you to cleanly separate your application code from your presentation. You can then offload some of your work and have time to concentrate on the Java code by handing styling duties over to a designer. Add the following entries to TimeEntry.css to implement your styles.

```
.timeEntryTable {
  padding-top: 35px;
}

.existingEntryTable {
  padding-top: 10px;
}

.separator {
  padding-left: 10px;
  padding-right: 10px;
}
```

You can add the class attributes for the styles above by using the addStyleName property for the various UI components. In the onModuleLoad method, you set the style for your flex table by adding the following:

```
flexEntryTable.setStylePrimaryName("timeEntryTable");
```

Modifying Your Hosted Page

One last modification before you run your modified application is to insert your new Root panel identifier. You need to modify TimeEntry.html and use your own HTML code instead of what is generated by the project wizard. Replace the code in the hosted page with the following:

```
<table align="center" width="1000">
    <tr>
      <td id="timeentryUI"></td>
    </tr>
      <tr>
        <td><img
src="http://code.google.com/appengine/images/appengine-noborder-120x30.gif"
alt="Powered by Google App Engine" style="padding-top: 20px"/></td>
      </tr>
```

```
    </table>
```

Running Your Application

Click the Run button again to launch your application in hosted mode. It should look like Figure 5-5.

Figure 5-5. *Your newly designed application*

Handling Client-Side Events

Like most web-based applications, your code executes based on user interaction. The user triggers some kind of event, such as a button click or a key press, and your application responds accordingly by performing some action. It shouldn't be a surprise to discover that GWT handles events with the same event-handler interface model that you find in other user-interface frameworks. A widget announces or publishes an event (for example, clicking a button), and other widgets subscribe to the event by receiving a particular event-handler interface and performing some action (for example, displaying a pop-up message).

Start by adding a click handler and an event listener for your Add Row button. You'll handle the Add Row button's click event by passing it an object that implements the ClickHandler interface. In the code below, you'll see that we use an anonymous inner class to implement ClickHandler. The interface has one method, onClick, which fires when the user clicks the button and adds a new row to the FlexTable for a new time entry.

```
// listen for mouse events on the add new row button
addRowButton.addClickHandler(new ClickHandler() {
    public void onClick(ClickEvent event) {
      addRow();
    }
});
```

One of your functional requirements is to allow users to record the amount of time they worked based on a user-defined start date. With your date picker you'll listen for changes to the selected date based on the interface's onValueChanged method. When the widget detects a change to its date, it sets the class variable to the widget's selected date, renames the columns of the FlexTable based on the start date, and displays the major visible components of the application.

```
// listen for the changes in the value of the date
dateBox.addValueChangeHandler(new ValueChangeHandler<Date>() {
        public void onValueChange(ValueChangeEvent<Date> evt) {
                startDate = evt.getValue();
                renameColumns();
                // show the main parts of the UI now
                flexEntryTable.setVisible(true);
                rightNav.setVisible(true);
                totalPanel.setVisible(true);
        }
});
```

Since the code above displays your major UI components when a date is selected by the date picker, you should add the code to hide the the components when the application initially loads. Add the following code before setting the Root panel in the onModuleLoad method.

```
// hide the main parts of the UI until they choose a date
flexEntryTable.setVisible(false);
rightNav.setVisible(false);
totalPanel.setVisible(false);
```

To track the date that the user selected in the addValueChangeHandler method above, you'll need to add another private instance variable called startDate.

```
private Date startDate;
```

Your preceding addValueChangeHandler method also calls a renameColumns method. To implement this method and its helper methods we need to have a quick discussion regarding date classes. Unfortunately, GWT doesn't support java.util.Calendar on the client and it doesn't appear that it will any time soon. Due to the way that individual browsers deal with dates, using dates on the client side with GWT is currently messy and involves using all of the deprecated methods of the java.util.Date class. Here is your renameColumns method along with the helper methods using the deprecated java.util.Date class methods.

```
private void renameColumns() {
        flexEntryTable.setText(0, 3, formatDate(startDate));
        flexEntryTable.setText(0, 4, formatDate(addDays(startDate,1)));
        flexEntryTable.setText(0, 5, formatDate(addDays(startDate,2)));
        flexEntryTable.setText(0, 6, formatDate(addDays(startDate,3)));
        flexEntryTable.setText(0, 7, formatDate(addDays(startDate,4)));
        flexEntryTable.setText(0, 8, formatDate(addDays(startDate,5)));
        flexEntryTable.setText(0, 9, formatDate(addDays(startDate,6)));
}

private Date addDays(Date d, int numberOfDays) {
        int day = d.getDate();
        int month = d.getMonth();
        int year = d.getYear();
        return new Date(year, month, day+numberOfDays);
}

private String formatDate(Date d) {
        return (d.getMonth()+1)+"/"+d.getDate()+"
("+d.toString().substring(0, 2)+")";
}
```

The last part of this chapter covers the FlexTable and how users enter their time. Each row has a text box for each day of the week, and you'll need to implement handlers and listeners to validate the data that the user enters. Add the following private class instance variables, which will allow you to track the row and column with which the user is currently interacting.

```
// tracks the current row and column in the grid
private int currentRow = 0;
private int currentColumn = 0;
```

Add a new event handler to the FlexTable and an anonymous inner class to implement ClickEvent. In this listener you want to determine the column and row for which the user is entering time. You'll use these values to total each row and validate user input.

```
flexEntryTable.addClickHandler(new ClickHandler(){
      public void onClick(ClickEvent event) {
            HTMLTable.Cell cellForEvent =
flexEntryTable.getCellForEvent(event);
            currentRow = cellForEvent.getRowIndex();
            currentColumn = cellForEvent.getCellIndex();
      }
});
```

Virtually every application requires validating user input to ensure valid parameters and data integrity. Your application is no different, however GWT is very weak in the validation department. A few frameworks can address this situation, but they are outside the scope of this book. You'll implement some simple validation using some standard and GWT components.

You need to ensure that the time that users enter are valid numbers and that they do not enter more than 24 hours for a single day. Instead of writing a series of listeners for each text box, you'll write a single handler and listener that will be shared by all data-entry text boxes.

```
private ValueChangeHandler<String> timeChangeHandler = new
ValueChangeHandler<String>() {
      public void onValueChange(ValueChangeEvent<String> evt) {

            try {
                  double t = Double.parseDouble(evt.getValue());
                  if (t > 24) {
                        Window.alert("You cannot work more than 24 hours
a day.");
                  } else {
                        totalRow();
```

```
                    }
             } catch (NumberFormatException e) {
                    TextBox tb = (TextBox)
flexEntryTable.getWidget(currentRow, currentColumn);
                    tb.setValue("0");
                    flexEntryTable.setWidget(currentRow, currentColumn, tb);
                    Window.alert("Not a valid number.");
             }

      }
};

day1.addValueChangeHandler(timeChangeHandler);
day2.addValueChangeHandler(timeChangeHandler);
day3.addValueChangeHandler(timeChangeHandler);
day4.addValueChangeHandler(timeChangeHandler);
day5.addValueChangeHandler(timeChangeHandler);
day6.addValueChangeHandler(timeChangeHandler);
day7.addValueChangeHandler(timeChangeHandler);
```

In the preceding timeChangeHandler method you make a call to total the current row's entries if the user enters a valid number that is less than 24. Your method loops through all of the time-entry TextBoxes for the current row, totals the amount, and then sets the display text widget for the row total. Since you've changed the total of the current row, you also want to update the total for the entire timecard. You make a call to totalGrid, which provides that functionality.

```
private void totalRow() {
      double rowTotal = 0.00;
      for (int cell = 3;cell<=9; cell++) {
             TextBox timeWidget = (TextBox)
flexEntryTable.getWidget(currentRow, cell);
             double t = Double.parseDouble(timeWidget.getValue());
             rowTotal = rowTotal + t;
      }
      flexEntryTable.setWidget(currentRow, 10, new
Label(NumberFormat.getFormat(".00").format(rowTotal)));
      totalGrid();
}
```

Totaling the entire timecard involves the summation of the rows in the FlexTable. Your method iterates over the current rows in the FlexTable (skipping the header row, of course) and sums the values in the row's total column. The grand total for the timecard is then displayed at the lower-right corner of the UI.

```
private void totalGrid() {
        double grandTotal = 0.00;
        for (int row=1;row<flexEntryTable.getRowCount();row++) {
                Label rowTotalWidget = (Label) flexEntryTable.getWidget(row,
10);
                double rowTotal =
Double.parseDouble(rowTotalWidget.getText());
                grandTotal = grandTotal + rowTotal;
        }
        ;
        totalLabel.setText(NumberFormat.getFormat(".00").format(grandTotal));
}
```

At this point your application's basic functionality is in place. The next couple of chapters will deal with authentication and persistence, so this is a good time to take a look at the entire code in the `TimeEntry.java` file (Listing 5-1).

Listing 5-1. The code for TimeEntry.java

```
package com.appirio.timeentry.client;

import com.google.gwt.core.client.EntryPoint;
import com.google.gwt.user.client.ui.Button;
import com.google.gwt.user.client.ui.FlexTable;
import com.google.gwt.user.client.ui.Label;
import com.google.gwt.user.client.ui.RootPanel;
import com.google.gwt.user.client.ui.VerticalPanel;
import com.google.gwt.user.client.ui.HorizontalPanel;
import com.google.gwt.user.client.ui.DockPanel;
import com.google.gwt.user.datepicker.client.DateBox;
import com.google.gwt.user.client.ui.AbsolutePanel;
import com.google.gwt.i18n.client.DateTimeFormat;
import com.google.gwt.user.client.ui.HasHorizontalAlignment;
import com.google.gwt.user.client.ui.Anchor;
import com.google.gwt.user.client.ui.Image;
import com.google.gwt.user.client.ui.DecoratedTabPanel;
import com.google.gwt.user.client.ui.ListBox;
import com.google.gwt.user.client.ui.TextBox;
import com.google.gwt.user.client.ui.CheckBox;
```

```java
import com.google.gwt.event.dom.client.ClickEvent;
import com.google.gwt.event.dom.client.ClickHandler;
import com.google.gwt.event.logical.shared.ValueChangeEvent;
import com.google.gwt.event.logical.shared.ValueChangeHandler;
import java.util.Date;
import com.google.gwt.user.client.ui.HTMLTable;
import com.google.gwt.user.client.Window;
import com.google.gwt.i18n.client.NumberFormat;


public class TimeEntry implements EntryPoint {

        private VerticalPanel mainPanel = new VerticalPanel();
        private AbsolutePanel totalPanel = new AbsolutePanel();
        private DockPanel navPanel = new DockPanel();
        private HorizontalPanel topPanel = new HorizontalPanel();

        private Label totalLabel = new Label("0.00");
        private FlexTable flexEntryTable = new FlexTable();
        private Image logo = new Image();

        // track the current row and column in the grid
        private int currentRow = 0;
        private int currentColumn = 0;
        private Date startDate;

        public void onModuleLoad() {

                logo.setUrl("images/appiriologo.png");

                HorizontalPanel userPanel = new HorizontalPanel();
                Anchor logOutLink = new Anchor("Sign Out");
                Label separator = new Label("|");
                separator.setStyleName("separator");
                userPanel.add(new Label("jeffdonthemic@gmail.com"));
                userPanel.add(separator);
                userPanel.add(logOutLink);

                topPanel.setWidth("1000px");
                topPanel.add(logo);
                topPanel.add(userPanel);
```

```
            topPanel.setCellHorizontalAlignment(userPanel,
HasHorizontalAlignment.ALIGN_RIGHT);

            // set up a horizontal panel to hold the date picker
            HorizontalPanel leftNav = new HorizontalPanel();
            leftNav.setSpacing(5);
            leftNav.add(new Label("Week Start Date"));
            DateBox dateBox = new DateBox();
            dateBox.setWidth("100px");
            dateBox.setFormat(new
DateBox.DefaultFormat(DateTimeFormat.getFormat("M/d/yyyy")));
            leftNav.add(dateBox);

            // set up a horizontal panel to hold the Add and Save buttons
            HorizontalPanel buttonPanel = new HorizontalPanel();
            buttonPanel.setSpacing(5);
            Button addRowButton = new Button("Add Row");
            Button saveButton = new Button("Save");
            buttonPanel.add(addRowButton);
            buttonPanel.add(saveButton);

            // set up another horizontal panel to dock all the buttons to
the right
            final HorizontalPanel rightNav = new HorizontalPanel();

      rightNav.setHorizontalAlignment(HasHorizontalAlignment.ALIGN_RIGHT);
            rightNav.setWidth("100%");
            rightNav.add(buttonPanel);

            // add all of the navigation panels to the dock panel
            navPanel.setWidth("1000px");
            navPanel.add(leftNav, DockPanel.WEST);
            navPanel.add(rightNav, DockPanel.EAST);

            // set up a horizontal panel to hold the grand total
            totalPanel.setSize("1000px","50px");
            totalPanel.add(new Label("Total:"), 900, 25);
            totalPanel.add(totalLabel, 950, 25);
```

```
            // listen for mouse events on the Add New Row button
            addRowButton.addClickHandler(new ClickHandler() {
                    public void onClick(ClickEvent event) {
                                    addRow();
                    }
            });

            // listen for the changes in the value of the date
            dateBox.addValueChangeHandler(new ValueChangeHandler<Date>() {
                    public void onValueChange(ValueChangeEvent<Date> evt) {
                            startDate = evt.getValue();
                            renameColumns();
                            // show the main parts of the UI now
                            flexEntryTable.setVisible(true);
                        rightNav.setVisible(true);
                        totalPanel.setVisible(true);
                    }
            });

            // set the width of the table to expand the size of the
navPanel
            flexEntryTable.setWidth("100%");

            // set the style for the table to be accessed in the css
            flexEntryTable.setStylePrimaryName("timeEntryTable");
            // add the columns and headers
            flexEntryTable.setText(0, 0, "Project");
            flexEntryTable.setText(0, 1, "Milestone");
            flexEntryTable.setText(0, 2, "Billable?");
            flexEntryTable.setText(0, 3, "Mon");
            flexEntryTable.setText(0, 4, "Tue");
            flexEntryTable.setText(0, 5, "Wed");
            flexEntryTable.setText(0, 6, "Thu");
            flexEntryTable.setText(0, 7, "Fri");
            flexEntryTable.setText(0, 8, "Sat");
            flexEntryTable.setText(0, 9, "Sun");
            flexEntryTable.setText(0, 10, "Total");

            VerticalPanel tab1Content = new VerticalPanel();
            tab1Content.add(navPanel);
            tab1Content.add(flexEntryTable);
            tab1Content.add(totalPanel);
```

```
        DecoratedTabPanel tabPanel = new DecoratedTabPanel();
        tabPanel.setWidth("100%");
        tabPanel.setAnimationEnabled(true);
        tabPanel.add(tab1Content, "Enter Time");
        tabPanel.selectTab(0);

        // add the navpanel and flex table to the main panel
        mainPanel.add(topPanel);
        mainPanel.add(tabPanel);
        // associate the main panel with the HTML host page.
        RootPanel.get("timeentryUI").add(mainPanel);

        addRow();

    }

    private void addRow() {

        int row = flexEntryTable.getRowCount();

        final ListBox lbMilestones = new ListBox(false);
        final ListBox lbProjects = new ListBox(false);
        lbProjects.addItem("-- Select a Project --");

        // create the time input fields for all 7 days
        final TextBox day1 = new TextBox();
        day1.setValue("0");
        day1.setWidth("50px");
        day1.setEnabled(false);
        final TextBox day2 = new TextBox();
        day2.setValue("0");
        day2.setWidth("50px");
        day2.setEnabled(false);
        final TextBox day3 = new TextBox();
        day3.setValue("0");
        day3.setWidth("50px");
        day3.setEnabled(false);
        final TextBox day4 = new TextBox();
        day4.setValue("0");
        day4.setWidth("50px");
        day4.setEnabled(false);
```

```
final TextBox day5 = new TextBox();
day5.setValue("0");
day5.setWidth("50px");
day5.setEnabled(false);
final TextBox day6 = new TextBox();
day6.setValue("0");
day6.setWidth("50px");
day6.setEnabled(false);
final TextBox day7 = new TextBox();
day7.setValue("0");
day7.setWidth("50px");
day7.setEnabled(false);

// add all of the widgets to the flex table
flexEntryTable.setWidget(row, 0, lbProjects);
flexEntryTable.setWidget(row, 1, lbMilestones);
flexEntryTable.setWidget(row, 2, new CheckBox());
flexEntryTable.setWidget(row, 3, day1);
flexEntryTable.setWidget(row, 4, day2);
flexEntryTable.setWidget(row, 5, day3);
flexEntryTable.setWidget(row, 6, day4);
flexEntryTable.setWidget(row, 7, day5);
flexEntryTable.setWidget(row, 8, day6);
flexEntryTable.setWidget(row, 9, day7);
flexEntryTable.setWidget(row, 10, new Label("0.00"));

flexEntryTable.addClickHandler(new ClickHandler(){
        public void onClick(ClickEvent event) {
                HTMLTable.Cell cellForEvent =
flexEntryTable.getCellForEvent(event);
                currentRow = cellForEvent.getRowIndex();
                currentColumn = cellForEvent.getCellIndex();
        }
});

day1.addValueChangeHandler(timeChangeHandler);
day2.addValueChangeHandler(timeChangeHandler);
day3.addValueChangeHandler(timeChangeHandler);
day4.addValueChangeHandler(timeChangeHandler);
day5.addValueChangeHandler(timeChangeHandler);
day6.addValueChangeHandler(timeChangeHandler);
day7.addValueChangeHandler(timeChangeHandler);
```

```
        }

        private void renameColumns() {
                flexEntryTable.setText(0, 3, formatDate(startDate));
                flexEntryTable.setText(0, 4,
formatDate(addDays(startDate,1)));
                flexEntryTable.setText(0, 5,
formatDate(addDays(startDate,2)));
                flexEntryTable.setText(0, 6,
formatDate(addDays(startDate,3)));
                flexEntryTable.setText(0, 7,
formatDate(addDays(startDate,4)));
                flexEntryTable.setText(0, 8,
formatDate(addDays(startDate,5)));
                flexEntryTable.setText(0, 9,
formatDate(addDays(startDate,6)));
        }

        private ValueChangeHandler<String> timeChangeHandler = new
ValueChangeHandler<String>() {
                public void onValueChange(ValueChangeEvent<String> evt) {

                        try {
                                double t = Double.parseDouble(evt.getValue());
                                if (t > 24) {
                                        Window.alert("You cannot work more than 24
hours a day.");
                                        TextBox tb = (TextBox)
flexEntryTable.getWidget(currentRow, currentColumn);
                                        tb.setValue("0");
                                        flexEntryTable.setWidget(currentRow,
currentColumn, tb);
                                } else {
                                        totalRow();
                                }
                        } catch (NumberFormatException e) {
                                TextBox tb = (TextBox)
flexEntryTable.getWidget(currentRow, currentColumn);
                                tb.setValue("0");
                                flexEntryTable.setWidget(currentRow,
currentColumn, tb);
```

```
                              Window.alert("Not a valid number.");
                      }

              }
      };

      private void totalRow() {
              double rowTotal = 0.00;
              for (int cell = 3;cell<=9; cell++) {
                      TextBox timeWidget = (TextBox)
flexEntryTable.getWidget(currentRow, cell);
                      double t = Double.parseDouble(timeWidget.getValue());
                      rowTotal = rowTotal + t;
              }
              flexEntryTable.setWidget(currentRow, 10, new
Label(NumberFormat.getFormat(".00").format(rowTotal)));
              totalGrid();
      }

      private void totalGrid() {
              double grandTotal = 0.00;
              for (int row=1;row<flexEntryTable.getRowCount();row++) {
                      Label rowTotalWidget = (Label)
flexEntryTable.getWidget(row, 10);
                      double rowTotal =
Double.parseDouble(rowTotalWidget.getText());
                      grandTotal = grandTotal + rowTotal;
              }
              ;

      totalLabel.setText(NumberFormat.getFormat(".00").format(grandTotal));
      }

      private Date addDays(Date d, int numberOfDays) {
              int day = d.getDate();
              int month = d.getMonth();
              int year = d.getYear();
              return new Date(year, month, day+numberOfDays);
      }

      private String formatDate(Date d) {
```

```
            return (d.getMonth()+1)+"/"+d.getDate()+"
("+d.toString().substring(0, 2)+")";
        }

}
```

Your front end is essentiallty complete. You'll make some minor tweaks in the upcoming chapters, but now you can focus your attention on the server side of your application.

Summary

In this chapter you got to work developing your application. You defined the functionality for your application as a standard timecard entry system that uses Google Accounts for authentication, Google Web Toolkit for presentation, and Bigtable for data persistence.

You started by creating your project in Eclipse and finished almost the entire front-end development by the end of the chapter. You got a good look at GWT and some of the features that make it an ideal platform for front-end development. A main advantage of GWT is that it hides the complexity of writing cross-browser JavaScript. You write your AJAX front-end in Java, which GWT then cross-compiles into optimized JavaScript that automatically works across all major browsers. The combination of the Eclipse plug-in and the hosted mode server are the "magic" that allows you to catch client-side exceptions in the Eclipse IDE instead of them popping up in the user's browser as a runtime exception.

During the course of the chapter you laid out your application and added custom styling to give it a nice look and feel. You then added all of your UI widgets and the handlers needed to respond to client-side events. At the end of the chapter you had all of the code necessary for your application's front end. In the next chapter we'll look at implementing authentication using Google Accounts.

CHAPTER 6

■ ■ ■

Authenticating Users

Nearly every web application nowadays requires user authentication of some sort, whether it's simply to change your e-mail address or manage your stock portfolio. Your application will be no different. You'll build out your authentication framework to let users enter and view timecard entries—naturally, only for themselves.

Authentication with App Engine comes in two flavors. You can choose to plug into Google's Accounts service (a.k.a Users service), or you can roll your own with custom classes, tables, and memcache. Developing your own authentication framework using memcache and sessions is fairly straightforward, but given the simplicity of Google Accounts, no one seems to do it. For most cases it just doesn't make sense to create a sign-up page, the ability to store user passwords, and add a "forgot my password" function, when you can use Google's code instead. You might want to make your own if you need to implement custom profiles and permissions, but typically you can just plug into Google Accounts and mark this requirement off your checklist. You'll get first-hand knowledge of the authentication functionality in Google Accounts because you'll be implementing this service for your application as well.

Introducing Google Accounts

Google Accounts is a mature and robust offering that currently boasts millions of active users. App Engine easily ties into this service and offers a smooth and familiar sign-in process for your users. There are cases when you may not want to use Google Accounts, but it is a quick and easy way to get users up and running with your application.

If your application is running under a Google Apps account, you can even use these Accounts features with members of your organization, eliminating the need to train users on how to create and manage their own accounts.

When your application utilizes the Google Accounts service, the Users API can determine whether the current user has signed in using her Google account. If she is not currently signed in, the service can redirect her to a sign-in page customized with text for your application, or it can allow her to create a new Google account. After the user signs in or creates an account, the service will redirect her back to your original page. Google takes care of generating the sign-in and sign-out URLs for you and can either display the URL to the user or automatically redirect them.

Another feature of the service is that it can distinguish admin users from regular users. So if the current user is an administrator for the application or a Google Apps user marked as an administrator, you can present them with an admin interface or another context specific to their profile. However, if you need to implement additional profiles, again, you will need to create your own authentication framework to achieve this level of functionality.

Restricting Access to Resources

In addition to restricting your entire application to authenticated users, you can specify access restrictions for certain URLs or URL paths based on the user's account. You configure access restrictions in the deployment descriptor by defining a series of <security-constraint> elements for URLs based on pattern matching. In addition to the URL, the security constraint also specifies the Google Accounts users or role. App Engine only supports * ("all users") and admin roles. It does not support custom security roles.

The process works the same as if you are restricting your entire application to authenticated users. If an unauthenticated user attempts to access a URL that matches a security constraint defined in the deployment descriptor, App Engine redirects him to the Google Accounts sign-in page. After he has logged in successfully, the service redirects him back to the original URL. Listing 6-1 provides a sample deployment descriptor using this approach.

Listing 6-1. *The web.xml deployment descriptor with security constraints*

```
<security-constraint>
    <web-resource-collection>
        <url-pattern>/myaccount/*</url-pattern>
    </web-resource-collection>
    <auth-constraint>
        <role-name>*</role-name>
    </auth-constraint>
</security-constraint>
```

```
<security-constraint>
    <web-resource-collection>
        <url-pattern>/private/*</url-pattern>
    </web-resource-collection>
    <auth-constraint>
        <role-name>admin</role-name>
    </auth-constraint>
</security-constraint>
```

■ **Note** Users must be signed in to your application before being granted access. If a user has signed in to a different application using a Google account, they are not authorized to access your application.

Users API

The Users API consists of a UserService, a User object, and a UserServiceFactory that creates a new UserService. Methods for the service and User object are described in Tables 6-1 and 6-2. In addition to the Users API, you can use the standard Servlet API and access the request object's getUserPrincipal() method to determine if the user has logged in with his Google account. The servlet can also access a user's e-mail address with getUserPrincipal.getName().

According to the documentation, App Engine supports storing the User object in Bigtable as its own special data type, however it does caution against using it as a stable identifier. You can add entities to the data store that contain a User object but querying with these identifiers returns no results. Google says that it may update this service to utilize this user type, but for now your best practice is to persist the user's e-mail address instead.

Table 6-1. *Methods in the UserService class*

Method	Description
createLoginURL	Returns a URL that can be used to display a login page to the user.
createLogoutURL	Returns a URL that can be used to log the current user out of this application.

Method	Description
getCurrentUser	If the user is logged in, this method will return a User that contains information about him.
isUserLoggedIn	Returns true if a user is logged in, otherwise returns false.

Table 6-2. *Major methods in the User class*

Method	Description
getNickname	Return this user's nickname. The nickname will be a unique, human- readable identifier (for example, an e-mail address) for this user with respect to this application. It will be an email address for some users, but not all.
getAuthDomain	Domain name into which this user has authenticated, or "gmail.com" for normal Google authentication.
getEmail	The user's e-mail address.

Development Mode

Google makes it easy to simulate its Accounts service by providing a dummy sign-in screen (see Figure 6-1) while you are developing your application. When your application requires authentication, it obtains a URL for the sign-in screen from the Users API. App Engine returns a special development URL and presents you with a dummy sign-in form that requires an e-mail address but no password. You can enter any e-mail address you'd like, and your application will execute just as it would if actually authenticating against Google Accounts. This sign-in screen also includes a check box so that you can simulate signing in as an administrator.

Once signed in, you can use the Users API to obtain a sign-out URL that cancels your dummy session.

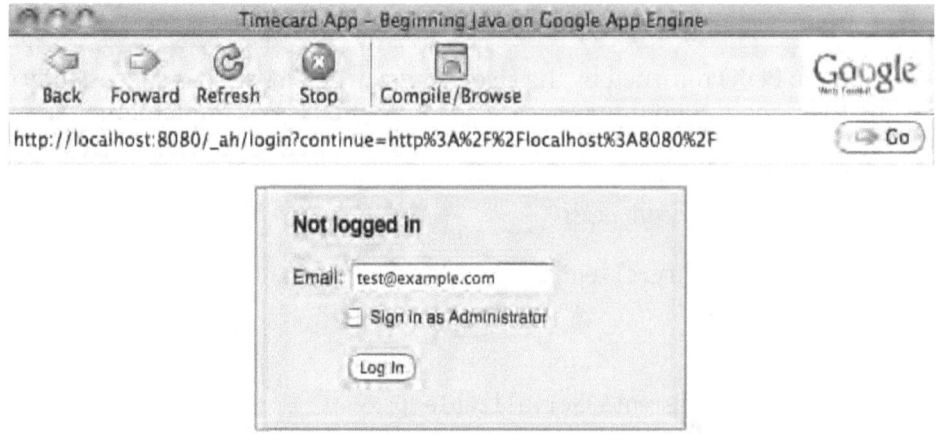

http://localhost:8080/_ah/login?continue=http%3A%2F%2Flocalhost%3A8080%2F

Figure 6-1. *The dummy sign-in screen*

Adding Authentication for Your Application

To authenticate your users, you will need to make a GWT remote procedure call to invoke the Users API. The GWT RPC framework simplifies the exchange of Java objects over the wire between your client and server components. Your client-side code will use GWT-generated proxy classes to make calls to your server-side service. These proxy objects will be serialized back and forth by GWT for method arguments and return values. To develop your login RPC service, you'll need to write the following four components:

- LoginInfo – An object that will contain the login info returned from the User service.

- LoginService - An interface that extends RemoteService and lists all of your RPC methods.

- LoginServiceImpl - A class that extends RemoteServiceServlet and implements the interface created in LoginService.

- LoginServiceAsync - The asynchronous interface for your service that is called by your client-side code.

LoginInfo Class

This class is a simple POJO returned by the User service when a user has successfully logged in using the Google Accounts service. The LoginInfo class is implemented in Listing 6-2.

Listing 6-2. *The code for LoginInfo.class*

```java
package com.appirio.timeentry.client;

import java.io.Serializable;

public class LoginInfo implements Serializable {

        private boolean loggedIn = false;
        private String loginUrl;
        private String logoutUrl;
        private String emailAddress;
        private String nickname;

        public boolean isLoggedIn() {
              return loggedIn;
        }

        public void setLoggedIn(boolean loggedIn) {
              this.loggedIn = loggedIn;
        }

        public String getLoginUrl() {
              return loginUrl;
        }

        public void setLoginUrl(String loginUrl) {
              this.loginUrl = loginUrl;
        }

        public String getLogoutUrl() {
              return logoutUrl;
        }

        public void setLogoutUrl(String logoutUrl) {
              this.logoutUrl = logoutUrl;
```

```
        }

        public String getEmailAddress() {
                return emailAddress;
        }

        public void setEmailAddress(String emailAddress) {
                this.emailAddress = emailAddress;
        }

        public String getNickname() {
                return nickname;
        }

        public void setNickname(String nickname) {
                this.nickname = nickname;
        }
}
```

LoginService and LoginServiceAsync Interfaces

Now you need to create two interfaces defining your login service and its methods.
In Listing 6-3 notice the "login" path annotation in the LoginService class. You'll
configure this path in the deployment descriptor to map the configuration to this
service.

Listing 6-3. *The code for LoginService.class*

```
package com.appirio.timeentry.client;

import com.google.gwt.user.client.rpc.RemoteService;
import com.google.gwt.user.client.rpc.RemoteServiceRelativePath;

@RemoteServiceRelativePath("login")
public interface LoginService extends RemoteService {
        public LoginInfo login(String requestUri);
}
```

Next, you need to add an AsyncCallback parameter to your service method. Your
interface in Listing 6-4 must be located in the same package as the service interface
and must also have the same name but appended with *Async*. Each method in this
interface must have the same name and signature as in the service interface

however, the method has no return type and the last parameter is an AsyncCallback object.

Listing 6-4. *The code for LoginServiceAsync.class*

```
package com.appirio.timeentry.client;

import com.google.gwt.user.client.rpc.AsyncCallback;

public interface LoginServiceAsync {
        public void login(String requestUri, AsyncCallback<LoginInfo> async);
}
```

Google Accounts Login Implementation

Now you need to create your server-side implementation (Listing 6-5) that uses Google Accounts to actually authenticate your users and return their information if successful.

Listing 6-5. *The code for LoginServiceImpl.class*

```
package com.appirio.timeentry.server;

import com.google.appengine.api.users.User;
import com.google.appengine.api.users.UserService;
import com.google.appengine.api.users.UserServiceFactory;
import com.appirio.timeentry.client.LoginInfo;
import com.appirio.timeentry.client.LoginService;
import com.google.gwt.user.server.rpc.RemoteServiceServlet;

public class LoginServiceImpl extends RemoteServiceServlet implements
        LoginService {

        public LoginInfo login(String requestUri) {
                LoginInfo loginInfo = new LoginInfo();
                UserService userService = UserServiceFactory.getUserService();
                User user = userService.getCurrentUser();

                if (user != null) {
                        loginInfo.setLoggedIn(true);

        loginInfo.setLogoutUrl(userService.createLogoutURL(requestUri));
```

```
                loginInfo.setNickname(user.getNickname());
                loginInfo.setEmailAddress(user.getEmail());
        } else {
                loginInfo.setLoggedIn(false);

    loginInfo.setLoginUrl(userService.createLoginURL(requestUri));
        }
        return loginInfo;
    }
}
```

Modifying the Deployment Descriptor

In your LoginService class you defined the "login" path annotation. Now you need to
add this definition to the deployment descriptor in Listing 6-6. You can also remove
the reference to greetServlet since it is not needed.

Listing 6-6. Servlet configuration to be added to the deployment descriptor

```
<servlet>
  <servlet-name>loginService</servlet-name>
  <servlet-class>com.appirio.timeentry.server.LoginServiceImpl</servlet-
class>
</servlet>

<servlet-mapping>
  <servlet-name>loginService</servlet-name>
  <url-pattern>/timeentry/login</url-pattern>
</servlet-mapping>
```

Modifying the User Interface

Now that your login RPC framework is in place, you need to tweak the client to allow
it to use your new authentication functionality. Currently, when your users load the
application, your timecard UI is immediately available. You need to change the flow
of the application to load the timecard UI if the user is already logged in or to redirect
them to the sign-in page if they are not. Once they sign-in with their Google account,
you'll still need to make a check to ensure that they are indeed authenticated.

You'll need to do some refactoring in TimeEntry.java to accomplish these tasks. In
Listing 6-7 you'll move the call to load the UI from the onModuleLoad method to a new

private method. You'll then add a new panel that displays the login form and modify onModuleLoad to display this panel conditionally.

First, rename the current onModuleLoad method to "loadMainUI" and make it private. Now add the following imports and methods to TimeEntry.java.

Listing 6-7. *Changes to TimeEntry.java*

```java
import com.google.gwt.core.client.GWT;
import com.google.gwt.user.client.rpc.AsyncCallback;

public void onModuleLoad() {

    logo.setUrl("images/appiriologo.png");

    LoginServiceAsync loginService = GWT.create(LoginService.class);
    loginService.login(GWT.getHostPageBaseURL(), new
AsyncCallback<LoginInfo>() {
        public void onFailure(Throwable error) {
        }

        public void onSuccess(LoginInfo result) {
            loginInfo = result;
            if(loginInfo.isLoggedIn()) {
                loadMainUI();
            } else {
                loadLoginUI();
            }
        }
    });

}

private void loadLoginUI() {
    VerticalPanel loginPanel = new VerticalPanel();
    Anchor loginLink = new Anchor("Sign In");
    loginLink.setHref(loginInfo.getLoginUrl());
    loginPanel.add(logo);
    loginPanel.add(new Label("Please sign-in with your Google Account to
access the Time Entry application."));
    loginPanel.add(loginLink);
    RootPanel.get("timeentryUI").add(loginPanel);
}
```

Now when your application loads, if users have not authenticated, they will see the sign-in page shown in Figure 6-2 as opposed to your timecard UI if they have already signed in.

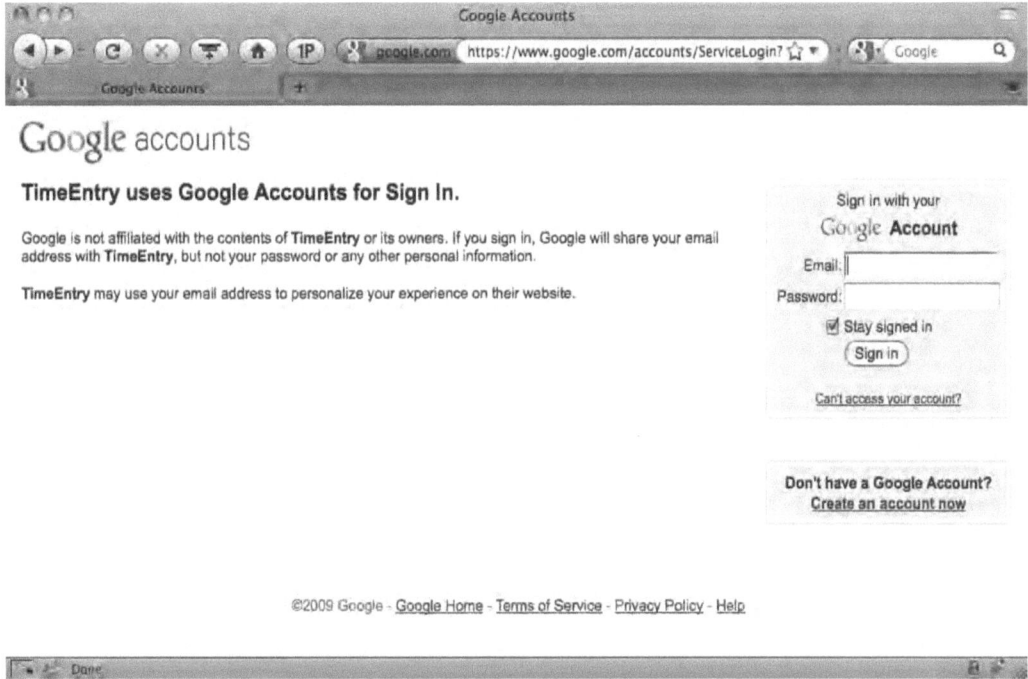

Figure 6-2. The Google Accounts sign-in page for your application

Summary

This chapter demonstrated how quick and easy it is to implement authentication for your timecard application using Google Accounts. The service offers role-based security to your application as well as individual directories.

App Engine is flexible and does not require you to use Google Accounts for authentication if it's not the best fiat for your application. If you need more granular security with customized permissions, you are free to develop your own framework using custom classes, tables, and memcache. However, doing so eliminates some of the development benefits that you get for free with Google Accounts.

CHAPTER 7

■■■

Using the App Engine Datastore

In the last couple of chapters we have focused on the client side of your application. You've developed the look and feel using GWT, and the authentication method that your application will utilize. Now it's time to move on to the server side, primarily your data integration layer.

In this chapter you'll get a detailed look at the App Engine datastore and you'll finish up the development of your application. At the end of this chapter you'll have a completed application that you can deploy to Google App Engine.

Introducing the App Engine Datastore

Designing highly scalable, data-intensive applications can be tricky. If you've ever used hardware or software load balancing, you know that your users can be interacting with any one of a dozen or so web and database servers. A user's request may not be serviced from the same server that handled his previous request. These servers could be spread out in different data centers or perhaps in different countries, requiring you to implement processes to keep your data safe, secure, and synchronized. The hardware and software required to scale your application can also be complex and expensive, and may even dictate that you outsource or hire dedicated resources.

With App Engine, Google takes care of everything for you. The App Engine datastore provides distribution, replication, and load-balancing services behind the scenes, freeing you up to focus on implementing your business logic. App Engine's datastore is powered mainly by two Google services: Bigtable and Google File System (GFS).).

Bigtable is a highly distributed and scalable service for storing and managing structured data. It was designed to scale to an extremely large size with petabytes of data across thousands of clustered commodity servers. It is the same service that Google uses for over 60 of its own projects including web indexing, Google Finance, and Google Earth.

The datastore also uses GFS to store data and log files. GFS is a scalable, fault-tolerant file system designed for large, distributed, data-intensive applications such as Gmail and YouTube. Originally developed to store crawling data and search indexes, GFS is now widely used to store user-generated content for numerous Google products.

Bigtable stores data as entities with properties organized by application-defined kinds such as customers, sales orders, or products. Entities of the same kind are not required to have the same properties or the same value types for the same properties. Bigtable queries entities of the same kind and can use filters and sort orders on both keys and property values. It also pre-indexes all queries, which results in impressive performance even with very large data sets. The service also supports transactional updates on single or application-defined groups of entities.

The first thing you'll notice about Bigtable is that it is not a relational database. Bigtable utilizes a non-relationship object model to store entities, allowing you to create simple, fast, and scalable applications. Google isn't alone in offering this type of architecture. Amazon's SimpleDB and many open-source datastores (for example, CouchDB and Hypertable) use this same approach, which requires no schema while providing auto-indexing of data and simple APIs for storage and access.

You can interact with Bigtable using either a standard API or a-low level API. With the standard API, either a Java Data Objects (JDO)) or Java Persistence API (JPA)) implementation, you can ensure that your applications are portable to other hosting providers and database technologies if you decide to jump ship. This makes a good argument for App Engine as it prevents vendor lock-in. If you are certain that your application will always run on App Engine, you can utilize the low-level API as it exposes the full capabilities of Bigtable. Both APIs achieve roughly the same results in terms of ability and performance, so it comes down to personal preference. Do you like working with low-level database functionality or abstracting this layer so that your experience is applicable across multiple datastore implementations?

The datastore provides full CRUD (create, read, update, and delete) access to entities in Bigtable and allows you to query against the datastore using a standard SQL-like query language called JDOQL. The syntax is enough like SQL to lull you into a sense of familiarity, but there are some differences when dealing with JDO-enhanced objects. One notable exception is the lack of support for joins, which is present in relational databases. However, this is understandable since the datastore is non-relational.

Working with Entities

The fundamental unit of data in the datastore is an "entity," which consists of an immutable identifier and zero or more properties. Once again, entities are schema-less and this allows for some interesting possibilities. Since entities are not required to have the same properties or types, your application must enforce adherence to your data model, whatever that may be at the time. A property can have one or more values, embedded classes, child objects, and even values of mixed types. Entities are very flexible and are not defined by a database schema as in a relational database. At any point during the application life cycle you can add or remove entity properties. Newly created and fetched entities will utilize this new schema. Your application's logic must be able to handle these changes.

App Engine uses the Java Persistence API (JPA)) and Java Data Objects (JDO)) interfaces for modeling and persisting entities. These APIs, rather than the low-level API, ensure application portability. For your application, you'll use JDO since the Eclipse plug-in generates your JDO configuration files. Of course, JPA is supported, but it requires some additional setup and configuration steps. If you are familiar with Hibernate or other object-relational mapping (ORM)) solutions, JDO should be fairly easy to grok as these solutions share many features.

App Engine's JDO implementation is provided by the DataNucleus Access Platform, an open-source implementation of JDO 2.3. Again, the JDO specification is database-agnostic and defines high-level interfaces for annotating simple POJOs, persisting and querying objects, and utilizing transactions. Applications implementing JDO can query for entities by property values or they can fetch a specific entity from the datastore using its key. Queries can return zero or more entities and sort them by property values, if desired.

Classes and Fields

JDO uses annotations on POJOs to describe how these objects are persisted to the datastore and how to recreate them when they are, in turn, fetched from the datastore. The kind of entity is defined by the simple name of the class while each class member specified as persistent represents a property of the entity. The data class is required to have a field dedicated to storing the primary key of its corresponding entity.

Each entity has a key that is unique to Bigtable. Keys consist of the application ID, the entity ID, and the kind of entity. Some keys may also contain information pertaining to the entity group. Your application can generate keys for your entities, or you can allow Bigtable to automatically assign numeric IDs for you. In most cases it is easier to let Bigtable assign your keys so you don't have to write code to ensure that your keys are unique across all objects of the same kind plus entity group parent (if being used).

There are four types of primary key fields:

1. *Long.* An ID that is automatically generated by Bigtable when the instance is saved.

2. *Uncoded String.* An ID or "key name" that your application provides to the instance prior to being saved.

3. *Key*: A value that includes the key of any entity-group parent that is being used and an application-generated string ID or a system-generated numeric ID.

4. *Key as Encoded String*: Essentially, an encoded key to ensure portability and still allow your application to take advantage of Bigtable's entity groups.

If you want to implement your own key system, you simply use the `createKey` static method of the `KeyFactory` class. You pass the method the kind and either an application-assigned string or a system-assigned number, and the method returns the appropriate Key instance. So, to create a key for an Order entity with the key name "jeff@noemail.com" you would use:

```
Key key = KeyFactory.createKey(Order.class.getSimpleName(),
"jeff@noemail.com");
```

■ **Note** If your implementation inadvertently creates a duplicate key for your entity, this new entity will overwrite the existing entity in the datastore.

Listing 7-1 is an example JDO class with an automatically generated Long ID provided by Bigtable with both persisted and non-persisted fields. The phone member is only available within the scope of the object and is not persisted to the database. Entities created from a database call will contain a null value for the phone member.

Listing 7-1. *Sample JDO POJO*

```
import javax.jdo.annotations.IdGeneratorStrategy;
import javax.jdo.annotations.IdentityType;
import javax.jdo.annotations.PersistenceCapable;
import javax.jdo.annotations.Persistent;
import javax.jdo.annotations.NotPersistent;
import javax.jdo.annotations.PrimaryKey;

// Declares the class as capable of being stored and retrieved with JDO
@PersistenceCapable(identityType = IdentityType.APPLICATION)
public class Contact {

        // Required primary key populated automatically by JDO
        @PrimaryKey
```

```
    @Persistent(valueStrategy = IdGeneratorStrategy.IDENTITY)
    private Long id;

    @Persistent
    private String name;

    // Field *NOT* persisted to the datastore
    @NotPersistent
    private String phone;

    public Contact(String name, String phone) {
        this.name = name;
        this.phone = phone;
    }

    // Accessors - used by your application but not JDO
    public Long getId() {
        return id;
    }

    public void setId(Long id) {
        this.id = id;
    }

    public String getName() {
        return name;
    }

    public void setName(String name) {
        this.name = name;
    }

    public String getPhone() {
        return phone;
    }

    public void setPhone(String phone) {
        this.phone = phone;
    }

}
```

The types of fields supported by JDO for entities include:

- Core types supported by Bigtable, as shown in Table 7-1

- An array of core datastore type values

- A Collection of core datastore type values

- @PersistenceCapable class instances or Collections

- Serializable class instances or Collections (stored as a Blob)

- Embedded classes that are stored as entity properties

As noted, a field value can be an instance of a class that is marked as @PersistenceCapable. A single instance creates a one-to-one relationship while a collection creates a one-to-many relationship. Using these types of relationships can dramatically increase object-modeling and code-writing productivity. For instance, you can create an Order class that defines an Address class as a persistent field. When your application creates an instance of the Order class, populates the address field with a new Address instance, and then saves the Order, the datastore will create both the Order and Address entities for you. The key of the Address entity has the key of the Order entity as its entity parent group.

Another object-modeling approach is to use embedded classes for persisting field values. With embedded classes the fields are stored directly in the datastore entity of the containing instance and do not exist as separate classes. Any data class marked as @PersistenceCapable can be used to embed in another data class. There is no need to specify a primary key field for the object as it is not stored as a self-referencing object.

```
@Persistent
@Embedded(members = {
    @Persistent(name="mailingAddress", columns=@Column(name="address1")),
    @Persistent(name="mailingCity", columns=@Column(name="city1")),
    @Persistent(name="mailingState", columns=@Column(name="state1")),
    @Persistent(name="mailingPostalCode",
columns=@Column(name="postalCode1")),
})
private Address address;
```

Since embedded classes are stored as part of the actual entity itself, you can use them with dot notation in JDOQL query filters and sort orders.

```
Select from Order Where address.mailingState = "KY"
```

Table 7-1. The Datastore Core Value Types

Type	Java Class	Notes
short text string, < 500 bytes	java.lang.String	
short byte string, < 500 bytes	com.google.appengine.api.datastore.ShortBlob	ShortBlob contains an array of bytes of a configurable length.
Boolean value	boolean or java.lang.Boolean	
integer	short, java.lang.Short, int, java.lang.Integer, long, java.lang.Long	Stored as a long integer, and then converted to the field type.
floating point number	float, java.lang.Float, double, java.lang.Double	Stored as a double-width float, and then converted to the field type.
date-time	java.util.Date	
Google account	com.google.appengine.api.users.User	User represents a specific user, represented by the combination of an e-mail address and a specific Google Apps domain.
long text string	com.google.appengine.api.datastore.Text	String of unlimited size.
long byte string	com.google.appengine.api.datastore.Blob	Blob contains an array of bytes of unlimited size.

Type	Java Class	Notes
entity key	com.google.appengine.api.datastore.Key, or the referenced object (as a child)	The primary key for a datastore entity. A datastore GUID.
a category	com.google.appengine.api.datastore.Category	A tag. For example, a descriptive word or phrase.
an e-mail address	com.google.appengine.api.datastore.Email	An RFC2822 e-mail address. Makes no attempt at validation.
a geographical point	com.google.appengine.api.datastore.GeoPt	A geographical point, specified by float latitude and longitude coordinates.
an instant messaging handle	com.google.appengine.api.datastore.IMHandle	An instant-messaging handle including both an address and its protocol.
a URL	com.google.appengine.api.datastore.Link	A URL with a limit of 2038 characters.
a phone number	com.google.appengine.api.datastore.PhoneNumber	A human-readable phone number. No validation is performed.
a postal address	com.google.appengine.api.datastore.PostalAddress	A human-readable mailing address. No validation is performed.

Type	Java Class	Notes
a user-provided rating, an integer between 0 to 100	com.google.appengine.api.datastore.Rating	A user-provided integer rating for a piece of content. Normalized to a 0-100 scale.

CRUDing Entities

With most datastores, obtaining a connection is an expensive process. The App Engine's datastore is no different. Applications utilizing JDO interact with the datastore by using an instance of the PersistenceManager class. By instantiating an instance of the PersistenceManagerFactory class, the factory creates an instance of the PersistenceManager using the JDO configuration. Due to the high overhead of creating the instance, you should wrap this class in a singleton so that it can be reused and prevented from creating additional instances.

```
import javax.jdo.JDOHelper;
import javax.jdo.PersistenceManagerFactory;

public final class PMF {
    private static final PersistenceManagerFactory pmfInstance =
        JDOHelper.getPersistenceManagerFactory("transactions-optional");

    private PMF() {}

    public static PersistenceManagerFactory get() {
        return pmfInstance;
    }
}
```

Creating Entities

Once you have a connection to the datastore, it's relatively simple to persist entities. Just create a new instance, and then pass it to the makePersistent synchronous method.

```
PersistenceManager pm = PMF.get().getPersistenceManager();
Order o = new Order("Jeff Douglas", "111-222-3333");
```

```
try {
    pm.makePersistent(o);
} finally {
    pm.close();
}
```

Fetching Entities

You can fetch an entity with its key by using the PersistenceManager's getObjectById method.

```
PersistenceManager pm = PMF.get().getPersistenceManager();
Key key = KeyFactory.createKey(Order.class.getSimpleName(),
"jeff@noemail.com");
Order o = pm.getObjectById(Order.class, key);
```

If you are using an encoded string ID or a numeric ID, you can fetch the entity by passing the getObjectById method the simple value of the key.

```
PersistenceManager pm = PMF.get().getPersistenceManager();
Order o = pm.getObjectById(Order.class, "jeff@noemail.com");
```

Updating Entities

You typically update an entity by fetching it with the PersistenceManager, make any changes to the instance, and then close the PersistenceManager. When the PersistenceManager is closed, it automatically updates any changes to the entity in the datastore, as the instance is said to be "attached" to the PersistenceManager.

```
public void updateOrder(Order order, String customerName) {
    PersistenceManager pm = PMF.get().getPersistenceManager();
    try {
        Order o = pm.getObjectById(Order.class, order.getId());
        o.setName(customerName);
    } finally {
        pm.close();
    }
}
```

Deleting Entities

Deleting an entity is relatively straightforward. Call the PersistenceManager's deletePersistent method with the object to delete. You can also delete multiple objects by calling the PersistenceManager's deletePersistentAll method with the Collection of objects. The delete action can also cascade down to any child objects, which can be deleted as well.

```
public void deleteOrder(Order order) {
    PersistenceManager pm = PMF.get().getPersistenceManager();
    try {
        Order o = pm.getObjectById(Order.class, order.getId());
        pm.deletePersistent(o);
    } finally {
        pm.close();
    }
}
```

Performing Queries with JDOQL

Now that you can perform basic CRUD functions, you'll need to be able to find entities that you'd like to take action on. JDO includes a SQL-like query language called JDOQL that performs queries for entities that meet specific sets of criteria. A JDOQL query specifies the entity kind to query, zero or more conditions or "filters" on entity properties, and zero or more sort-order descriptions. JDOQL also performs type checking for results and query parameters to make life easier.

The query API is very accommodating and allows you to mix and match your JDOQL query string to suit your preferences. You can write your entire JDOQL query as a single string or construct all or some of the query by calling methods on the query object with filters and parameter substitutions in the order in which they are declared. Literal values are also supported for string and numeric values.

Here is a simple query constructed with the JDOQL string syntax:

```
import java.util.List;
import javax.jdo.Query;

Query qry = pm.newQuery("select from Contact where country == countryParam " +
        "order by dateCreated desc " +
        "parameters String countryParam");

List<Contact> contacts = (List<Contact>) qry.execute("USA");
```

Here is the same query using the method style of calling. This method is a little more straightforward and is easier to maintain than the string format.

```
Query qry = pm.newQuery(Contact.class);
qry.setFilter("country == countryParam");
qry.setOrdering("dateCreated desc");
qry.declareParameters("String countryParam");

List<Contact> contacts = (List<Contact>) qry.execute("USA");
```

Again, JDOQL is very flexible. You can mix these two styles according to your business requirements to create some interesting and dynamic combinations.

```
Query qry = pm.newQuery(Contact.class,
        "country == countryParam order by dateCreated desc");
qry.declareParameters("String countryParam");

List<Contact> contacts = (List<Contact>) qry.execute("USA");
```

Filtering Queries

Queries can contain zero or more filters specifying a field name, an operator, and a value. Values cannot refer to another property or be calculated in terms of other properties. Your application must provide the values for the filters. JDOQL supports only the following filter operators: <, <=, ==, >=, and >.

When using the JDOQL string syntax, you can only use && (logical "and") to separate your filters. The datastore does not support other combinations (for example, "or", "not").

Another restriction for queries pertains to inequality filters. You must not construct your queries to contain inequality filters on more than one property. However, the same property may contain multiple inequality filters, as shown in this example.

```
qry.setFilter("countryName == 'USA' && stateName == stateName");
qry.declareParameters("String stateName");
```

Sorting Queries

The results of a JDOQL query can be sorted based on a property and a direction, either ascending or descending. If a sort order is not specified, then the results of the query are returned in the order of their entity keys.

As with filters, there are some restrictions on the sorting that can be performed. If your query includes sort orders on some properties and inequality filters on other properties, then the property that includes the inequality filters must be ordered before the other properties. Here is a short example of sorting by multiple properties.

```
qry.setOrdering("dateCreated desc, stateName asc");
```

Query Ranges

Your JDOQL queries can specify a range of entities to be returned to your application. The setRange method accepts numeric indexes for the first and last entities that should be included in the resultset. The index is zero-based, so given the query below, the third, fourth, and fifth entities will be returned in the results.

```
qry.setRange(2,5);
```

Using ranges can be resource-intensive because the datastore returns all entities and then discards the ones prior to the starting index. Use ranges with care for large data sets.

You might be tempted to use ranges to implement pagination for your application. However, App Engine recommends a slightly different approach, as discussed in the article, "Paging through large datasets" (http://code.google.com/appengine/articles/paging.html).

Using Indexes

For performance and scalability, the datastore maintains an index for each query that your application can execute. An index is built as a combination of each kind, filter property and operator, and sort order for every query in your application. As changes are made to your entities in the datastore, the datastore automatically updates its indexes with the correct results. When a JDOQL query is executed, the datastore returns the results directly from its corresponding index.

Scanning Google Groups you will find that there is much uncertainty surrounding indexes and how they are built. You can either define them manually in the datastore-index.xml configuration file, or the development web server *may* create them for you.

Building Indexes

At runtime, if App Engine executes a query with no corresponding index, it will fail miserably. By default, App Engine builds a number of simple indexes for you. For more complex indexes, you will have to build them manually in the index configuration file, as shown in Listing 7-2.

Listing 7-2. *Sample datastore-index.xml file*

```
<?xml version="1.0" encoding="utf-8"?>
<datastore-indexes
  xmlns="http://appengine.google.com/ns/datastore-indexes/1.0"
  autoGenerate="true">
      <datastore-index kind="Contact" ancestor="false">
            <property name="countryName" direction="asc" />
      </datastore-index>
</datastore-indexes>
```

Indexes are built automatically by App Engine for queries that contain:

- Single property inequality filters

- Only one property sort order (ascending or descending) and no filters

- Inequality or range filters on keys and equality filters on properties

- Only ancestor and equality filters

You must specify in the index configuration file any queries containing:

- Multiple sort orders

- Inequality and ancestor filters

- A sort order on multiple keys in descending order

- One or more inequality filters on a property and one or more equality filters over the properties

Creating Indexes In Development Mode

During development, App Engines tries to create your indexes for you in the configuration file. If the development web server encounters a query that does not have a corresponding index, it will try to create an index for you automatically. If your unit tests call every possible query for your application, the generated configuration file will contain a complete set of all indexes. This is where confusion creeps into the process. If you think your tests call all possible queries but your application still fails at runtime, you'll have to edit the datastore-index.xml file and add these indexes manually.

Using Transactions

At a high level, the App Engine datastore supports transactions like most relational databases. A transaction consists of one or more database operations that either succeed or fail in entirety. If a transaction succeeds, then all operations are committed to the datastore. However, if one of the operations fails, then all operations are rolled back to their original state. An example method using transactions is shown in Listing 7-3.

Listing 7-3. Sample transaction

```
import javax.jdo.Transaction;

public void createContact(Contact contact, String accountId) {

        PersistenceManager pm = PMF.get().getPersistenceManager();
        Transaction tx = pm.currentTransaction();

        try {
                // start the transaction
                tx.begin();

                // persist the contact
                pm.makePersistent(contact);

                // fetch the parent account
                Account account = pm.getObjectById(Account.class, accountId);
                account.incrementContacts(1);
                pm.makePersistent(account);

                // commit if no errors
                tx.commit();
        } finally {

                // roll back the transactions in case of an error
                if (tx.isActive()) {
                        tx.rollback();
                }

        }
}
```

All entities in the datastore belong to an entity group. Entities in the same group are stored in the same part of Google's distributed network. Better distribution across database nodes improves performance when creating and updating data. When creating a new entity, you can assign an existing entity as its parent so that the new entity becomes part of that entity group. If you do not specify a parent for an entity, it is considered a root entity.

The datastore places restrictions on what operations can be performed inside a single transaction:

- Your application can perform a query inside a transaction but only if the query includes an ancestor filter to retrieve all descendants of the specific entity.

- A transaction must operate only on entities in the same entity group.

- If your transaction fails, your application must try again programmatically. JDO will not attempt to retry the transaction automatically, like most systems with optimistic concurrency.

- A transaction can only update an entity once.

Finishing Up Your Application

Now that you have a good understanding of the App Engine datastore and how to use JDO to interact with it, you can finish up the application. You'll need to tie various parts of your application into the datastore using GWT RPC to create a fully functioning application, following these steps:

- Populate your Projects picklist with values.

- Populate your Milestones picklist with values based on the selected project.

- Implement your Save handler to persist your timecard entries to the datastore.

- Display the current user's timecard entries from the datastore.

Making Remote Procedure Calls with GWT RPC

Similar to your authentication service, your data service will use GTW RPC to communicate with your server (see Figure 7-1). You'll create a server-side service that is invoked by your client to fetch and save timecard entries and related project information. You will need to implement the following components to round out your application:

1. A server-side service containing the methods that your client will invoke

2. The client-side code that will invoke the service

3. A serializable POJO containing your actual timecard data that is passed between your server and client

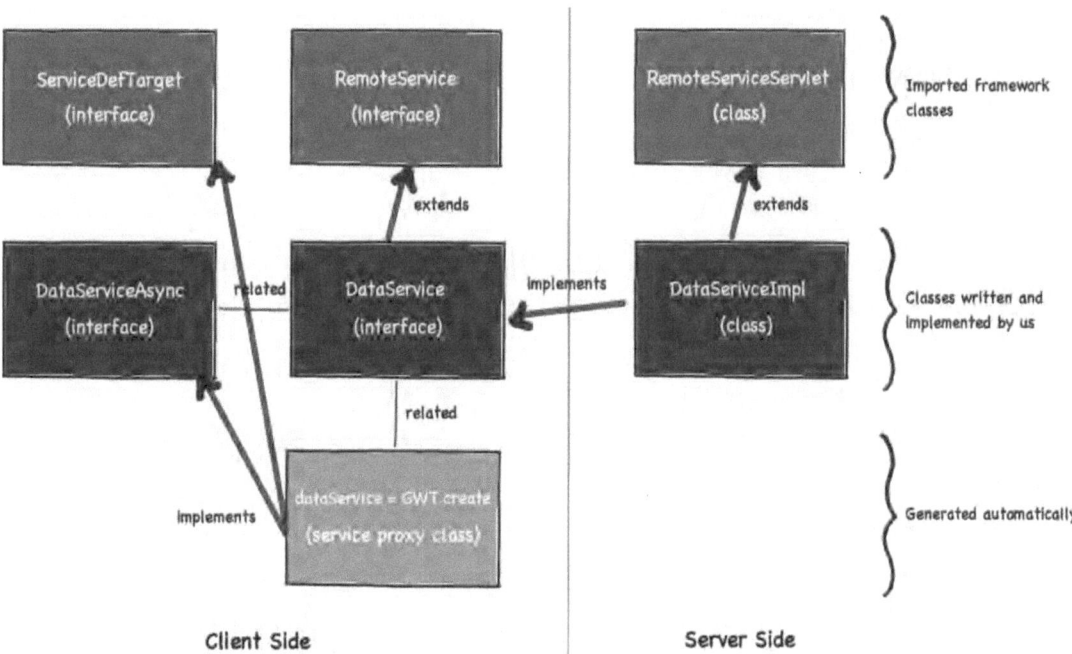

Figure 7-1. Your GWT RPC components model

TimeEntryData POJO

Your client and server will need a POJO to pass data back and forth. The POJO in Listing 7-4 will be a single timecard entry that will be persisted to the datastore. When using GWT RPC, the class, parameters, and return types must be serializable so that the object can be moved from layer to layer.

Listing 7-4. The TimeEntryData POJO

```java
package com.appirio.timeentry.client;

import java.io.Serializable;
import java.util.Date;

public class TimeEntryData implements Serializable {

        private String project;
        private String milestone;
        private Boolean billable;
        private Date date;
        private double hours;

        public String getProject() {
                return project;
        }

        public void setProject(String project) {
                this.project = project;
        }

        public String getMilestone() {
                return milestone;
        }

        public void setMilestone(String milestone) {
                this.milestone = milestone;
        }

        public Boolean getBillable() {
                return billable;
        }

        public void setBillable(Boolean billable) {
                this.billable = billable;
        }

        public Date getDate() {
                return date;
        }
```

```
    public void setDate(Date date) {
        this.date = date;
    }

    public double getHours() {
        return hours;
    }

    public void setHours(double hours) {
        this.hours = hours;
    }

}
```

■ **Note** GWT serialization is a little different from the Java Serializable interface. Check out the GWT Developer's Guide for details on the differences and reasons behind them.

TimeEntryEntity JDO Class

Your TimeEntryData POJO is transferred across the wire to your server and is deserialized automatically. For flexibility, you're going to create the JDO class in Listing 7-5 for persisting your instances to the datastore.

Listing 7-5. The code for your JDO class, TimeEntryEntity.java

```
package com.appirio.timeentry.server;

import javax.jdo.annotations.IdGeneratorStrategy;
import javax.jdo.annotations.IdentityType;
import javax.jdo.annotations.PersistenceCapable;
import javax.jdo.annotations.Persistent;
import javax.jdo.annotations.PrimaryKey;
import java.util.Date;

@PersistenceCapable(identityType = IdentityType.APPLICATION)
public class TimeEntryEntity {

    @PrimaryKey
    @Persistent(valueStrategy = IdGeneratorStrategy.IDENTITY)
```

```java
private Long id;
@Persistent
private String email;
@Persistent
private String project;
@Persistent
private String milestone;
@Persistent
private Boolean billable;
@Persistent
private Date date;
@Persistent
private double hours;

public Long getId() {
    return id;
}

public void setId(Long id) {
    this.id = id;
}

public String getEmail() {
    return email;
}

public void setEmail(String email) {
    this.email = email;
}

public String getProject() {
    return project;
}

public void setProject(String project) {
    this.project = project;
}

public String getMilestone() {
    return milestone;
}
```

```java
    public void setMilestone(String milestone) {
        this.milestone = milestone;
    }

    public Boolean getBillable() {
        return billable;
    }

    public void setBillable(Boolean billable) {
        this.billable = billable;
    }

    public Date getDate() {
        return date;
    }

    public void setDate(Date date) {
        this.date = date;
    }

    public double getHours() {
        return hours;
    }

    public void setHours(double hours) {
        this.hours = hours;
    }

}
```

NotLoggedIn Exception

When interacting with the datastore, your service needs to ensure that the user is logged in to the application with her Google account. If the user has not logged in or her session has expired, you need to handle this by throwing the NotLoggedInException shown in Listing 7-6.

Listing 7-6. The code for the NotLoggedInException

```java
package com.appirio.timeentry.client;

import java.io.Serializable;
```

```
public class NotLoggedInException extends Exception implements Serializable
{

    public NotLoggedInException() {
        super();
    }

    public NotLoggedInException(String message) {
        super(message);
    }

}
```

Creating Your Data Service

In order to create your data service for your server, you need to define both a service interface and the actual service. For your service interface you need to define the interface extending the GWT RemoteService interface,GWT RemoteService interface, as shown in Listing 7-7. Your service will consist of the following methods that will be called from your client:

1. *getProjects*: Returns an Array of Strings for the Project picklist

2. *getMilestones*: Accepts a project name and returns an Array of Strings for the Milestones picklist

3. *addEntries*: Accepts a Vector of TimeEntryData objects and returns a String with the results of the datastore commit

4. *getEntries*: Returns a Vector of TimeEntryData objects containing the current timecard entries for the current user

Listing 7-7. *Your data service extending the GWT RemoteService*

```
package com.appirio.timeentry.client;

import java.util.Vector;

import com.google.gwt.user.client.rpc.RemoteService;
import com.google.gwt.user.client.rpc.RemoteServiceRelativePath;
import com.appirio.timeentry.client.TimeEntryData;

@RemoteServiceRelativePath("data")
public interface DataService extends RemoteService {
```

```
      String[] getProjects();
      String[] getMilestones(String project);
      String addEntries(Vector<TimeEntryData> entries) throws
NotLoggedInException;
      Vector<TimeEntryData> getEntries() throws NotLoggedInException;
}
```

■ **Note** Notice the @RemoteServiceRelativePath annotation. You'll define this path in the deployment descriptor based on the relative path of the base URL.

The guts of your service reside in the DataServiceImpl class shown in Listing 7-8. The methods defined in your interface are implemented in addition to a number of helper methods. This class extends GWT RemoteServiceServlet and does the heavy lifting of serializing responses and deserializing requests for you. Since the servlet runs as Java bytecode instead of JavaScript on the client, you are not hamstrung by the functionality of the browser.

Listing 7-8. The entire listing for DataServiceImpl.java

```
package com.appirio.timeentry.server;

import java.util.List;
import java.util.Vector;
import java.util.logging.Logger;
import java.util.logging.Level;

import javax.jdo.PersistenceManager;
import javax.jdo.PersistenceManagerFactory;
import javax.jdo.JDOHelper;

import com.google.appengine.api.users.User;
import com.google.appengine.api.users.UserService;
import com.google.appengine.api.users.UserServiceFactory;
import com.appirio.timeentry.client.NotLoggedInException;

import com.appirio.timeentry.client.DataService;
import com.appirio.timeentry.client.TimeEntryData;
import com.google.gwt.user.server.rpc.RemoteServiceServlet;
```

```java
@SuppressWarnings("serial")
public class DataServiceImpl extends RemoteServiceServlet implements
DataService {

    private static final Logger LOG =
Logger.getLogger(DataServiceImpl.class.getName());
    private static final PersistenceManagerFactory PMF =
JDOHelper.getPersistenceManagerFactory("transactions-optional");


    public String addEntries(Vector<TimeEntryData> entries) throws
NotLoggedInException {

        // ensure that the current user is logged in
        checkLoggedIn();

        PersistenceManager pm = getPersistenceManager();
        try {
            pm.makePersistentAll(toEntities(entries));
        } finally {
            pm.close();
        }
        LOG.log(Level.INFO, entries.size()+" entries added.");
        return entries.size()+" entries added.";
    }

    public Vector<TimeEntryData> getEntries() throws NotLoggedInException
{

        // ensure that the current user is logged in
        checkLoggedIn();

        Vector<TimeEntryData> entries = new Vector<TimeEntryData>();

        PersistenceManager pm = getPersistenceManager();
        try {
            String query = "select from " +
TimeEntryEntity.class.getName() + " where email == '"+ getUser().getEmail()
+"' order by date desc";
            List<TimeEntryEntity> entities = (List<TimeEntryEntity>)
pm.newQuery(query).execute();
```

```java
                for (TimeEntryEntity entity : entities) {
                        TimeEntryData ted = new TimeEntryData();
                        ted.setBillable(entity.getBillable());
                        ted.setDate(entity.getDate());
                        ted.setHours(entity.getHours());
                        ted.setMilestone(entity.getMilestone());
                        ted.setProject(entity.getProject());
                        entries.add(ted);
                }

        } finally {
                pm.close();
        }

        return entries;
}

// returns a simple String Array of project names
public String[] getProjects() {

        String[] projects = new String[3];
        projects[0] = "Project 1";
        projects[1] = "Project 2";
        projects[2] = "Project 3";

        return projects;
}

// returns a simple String Array of milestone name for a project
public String[] getMilestones(String project) {

        String[] milestones = new String[3];

        if (project.equals("Project 1")) {
                milestones[0] = "Milestone 1-1";
                milestones[1] = "Milestone 1-2";
                milestones[2] = "Milestone 1-3";
        } else if (project.equals("Project 2")) {
                milestones[0] = "Milestone 2-1";
                milestones[1] = "Milestone 2-2";
                milestones[2] = "Milestone 2-3";
```

```
        } else {
                milestones[0] = "Milestone 3-1";
                milestones[1] = "Milestone 3-2";
                milestones[2] = "Milestone 3-3";
        }

        return milestones;
    }

    private PersistenceManager getPersistenceManager() {
        return PMF.getPersistenceManager();
    }

    // returns the current user from Google Accounts
    private User getUser() {
        UserService userService = UserServiceFactory.getUserService();
        return userService.getCurrentUser();
    }

    // determines if the user is currently logged in. If not, throws an
exception.
    private void checkLoggedIn() throws NotLoggedInException {
        if (getUser() == null)
                throw new NotLoggedInException("User not logged in.
Please login with your Google Accounts credentials.");
    }

    // utility method to translate client objects to server-side objects
    private Vector<TimeEntryEntity> toEntities(Vector<TimeEntryData>
entries) {
        // create a new vector of entities to return
        Vector<TimeEntryEntity> entities = new
Vector<TimeEntryEntity>();
        for (int i=0;i<entries.size();i++) {
                TimeEntryData ted = (TimeEntryData) entries.get(i);
                TimeEntryEntity tee = new TimeEntryEntity();
                tee.setBillable(ted.getBillable());
                tee.setDate(ted.getDate());
                tee.setHours(ted.getHours());
                tee.setMilestone(ted.getMilestone());
                tee.setProject(ted.getProject());
                tee.setEmail(getUser().getEmail());
```

```
                entities.add(tee);
            }
            return entities;
        }

}
```

Modifying the Deployment Descriptor

Since your service implementation runs on the server as a servlet, you need to tell the embedded Servlet container where to find the code to execute. Open the web.xml file in the project's war directory and add the entries in Listing 7-9. The URL pattern for the dataServlet corresponds to the @RemoteServiceRelativePath("data") annotation in the DataService interface that you added earlier.

Listing 7-9. *The web.xml definition for the DataServiceImpl servlet*

```
<servlet>
  <servlet-name>dataServlet</servlet-name>
  <servlet-class>com.appirio.timeentry.server.DataServiceImpl</servlet-
class>
</servlet>

<servlet-mapping>
  <servlet-name>dataServlet</servlet-name>
  <url-pattern>/timeentry/data</url-pattern>
</servlet-mapping>
```

Invoking the Service from the GWT Client

Now that the server side of your application is complete, you need to implement the client-side code that invokes your service. Before you make your modifications to your EntryPoint class, you need to add one more component for your GWT RPC calls.

You need to add an AsyncCallback parameter to each of your server-side calls for your DataService. Your new interface in Listing 7-10 must be located in the same package as your service interface and it must have the same name as the interface but appended with *Async.*

Listing 7-10. The code for DataServiceAsync

```
package com.appirio.timeentry.client;

import java.util.Vector;

import com.appirio.timeentry.client.TimeEntryData;
import com.google.gwt.user.client.rpc.AsyncCallback;

public interface DataServiceAsync {
        void getProjects(AsyncCallback<String[]> callback);
        void getMilestones(String project, AsyncCallback<String[]> callback);
        void addEntries(Vector<TimeEntryData> entries, AsyncCallback<String>
callback);
        void getEntries(AsyncCallback<Vector<TimeEntryData>> callback);
}
```

The first thing you need to do before you can start making RPC calls to your server is to create an instance of the service proxy class. Add the following private class member to your EntryPoint class, TimeEntry.java.

```
private final DataServiceAsync dataService = GWT.create(DataService.class);
```

With your dataService proxy defined you can start integrating your data from the datastore into your client. Add the code in Listing 7-11 at the end of the addRow method. This new code interacts with your server in two important ways. Whenever a new row is added to the FlexTable, the getProjects method makes an RPC call to fetch all of the projects from the server, and then populates the values in the picklist. The inline AsyncCallback object contains two methods, onSuccess and onFailure, the appropriate one of which is called depending on whether the RPC call succeeds or fails.

The code also adds a listener to the Project picklist that detects changes in the selected value. When a user selects a project from the picklist, the getMilestones RPC RPC method is called and fetches the appropriate milestones. If the call succeeds, the resulting milestones populate the values in the Milestone picklist and the seven time input boxes are enabled for entry.

Listing 7-11. Code added to the addRow method in TimeEntry.java

```
// get all of the projects for the user
dataService.getProjects(new AsyncCallback<String[]>() {

        public void onFailure(Throwable caught) {
            handleError(caught);
```

```
        }

        public void onSuccess(String[] results) {
            for (int i=0;i<results.length;i++)
                    lbProjects.addItem(results[i]);
        }
});


lbProjects.addChangeHandler(new ChangeHandler () {
      public void onChange(ChangeEvent event) {

            // remove all of the current items in the milestone list

            for (int i=lbMilestones.getItemCount()-1;i>=0;i--)

                    lbMilestones.removeItem(i);

            // get all of the milestones for the project

        dataService.getMilestones(lbProjects.getItemText(lbProjects.getSelect
edIndex()), new AsyncCallback<String[]>() {

                        public void onFailure(Throwable caught) {
                                handleError(caught);
                        }

                        public void onSuccess(String[] results) {
                                for (int i=0;i<results.length;i++)
                                        lbMilestones.addItem(results[i]);

                                day1.setEnabled(true);
                                day2.setEnabled(true);
                                day3.setEnabled(true);
                                day4.setEnabled(true);
                                day5.setEnabled(true);
                                day6.setEnabled(true);
                                day7.setEnabled(true);
                        }
                });

      }
});
```

The onFailure method of your AsyncCallback object references a small helper method to display any error returned from the server. Add this method to your class along with some required import statements.

```
import com.google.gwt.event.dom.client.ChangeEvent;
import com.google.gwt.event.dom.client.ChangeHandler;
import java.util.Vector;

private void handleError(Throwable error) {
    Window.alert(error.getMessage());
    if (error instanceof NotLoggedInException)
        Window.Location.replace(loginInfo.getLogoutUrl());

}
```

Your time-entry UI is almost complete. Users can now add rows to their timecards, select projects and milestones, and enter their time for the appropriate days. Your last major task for entering time is writing the entries to the datastore. To perform this function you'll add the code in Listing 7-12.

The saveEntries method gathers up all of the user-entered timecard data rows into a Vector of TimeEntryData objects. If there are any timecard entries to submit to the server, the Vector of objects is passed to the server, the entries are persisted to the datastore, and the results are sent back and displayed to the user in a standard JavaScript Alert window.

Listing 7-12. *Code for the saveEntries method*

```
private void saveEntries() {

        Vector<TimeEntryData> entries = new Vector<TimeEntryData>();

        for (int row=1;row<flexEntryTable.getRowCount();row++) {

                ListBox projectWidget = (ListBox)
flexEntryTable.getWidget(row, 0);
                ListBox milestoneWidget = (ListBox)
flexEntryTable.getWidget(row, 1);
                CheckBox billableWidget = (CheckBox)
flexEntryTable.getWidget(row, 2);
```

```
            for (int column=3;column<10;column++) {
                // get the current text box for the day
                TextBox textBox = (TextBox)
flexEntryTable.getWidget(row, column);
                double hours = Double.parseDouble(textBox.getValue());
                if (hours > 0) {
                    TimeEntryData ted = new TimeEntryData();
                    ted.setHours(hours);

        ted.setMilestone(milestoneWidget.getItemText(
                            milestoneWidget.getSelectedIndex()));
                    ted.setProject(projectWidget.getItemText(
                        projectWidget.getSelectedIndex()));
                    ted.setBillable(billableWidget.getValue());
                    ted.setDate(addDays(startDate,(column-3)));
                    entries.add(ted);
                }
            }

        }

        if (!entries.isEmpty()) {

            // submit the entries to the server
            dataService.addEntries(entries, new AsyncCallback<String>() {

                public void onFailure(Throwable caught) {
                        handleError(caught);
                }

                public void onSuccess(String message) {
                        Window.alert(message);
                }
            });
        }
}
```

One thing you still need to do is add the click event to the Save button to call this new saveEntries method method. Add the following code to the loadLoginUI method:

```
// listen for mouse events on the save button
saveButton.addClickHandler(new ClickHandler() {
```

```
        public void onClick(ClickEvent event) {
                saveEntries();
                removeAllRows();
        }
});
```

After you save the entries to the server, your code needs to remove all of the current timecard entries and present the user with a FlexTable that contains only one blank row for new data entry. Add the following method to the TimeEntry class.

```
private void removeAllRows() {
        // remove all of the rows from the flex table
        for (int row=flexEntryTable.getRowCount()-1;row>0;row--)
                flexEntryTable.removeRow(row);

        // rest the total
        totalLabel.setText("0.00");
        // add a new blank row to the flex table
        addRow();
}
```

Displaying Timecard Entries

Now your timecard entry UI is complete! However, one of your functional requirements was to display the user's current timecard entries. You'll add another tab to your UI and display a simple FlexTable with all of the user's current entries. Remember, you already implemented the server-side code earlier in this chapter.

Start by adding a new FlexTable to hold all of the existing timecard entries. Add the following private class member.

```
private FlexTable flexCurrentTable = new FlexTable();
```

Now simply add another tab titled "Current Entries" to the DecoratedTabPanel with your newly created FlexTable.

```
tabPanel.add(flexCurrentTable,"Current Entries");
```

There's only one function of your new FlexTable: display entries for the current user. To populate the FlexTable with data from the server, you need to implement the following getCurrentEntries method in Listing 7-13 that makes an RPC call to the server and fetches the user's current entries. The method doesn't need to pass any type of user indentifier as the implementation on the server simply references the user's data from their Google account.

Listing 7-13. *Code for the getCurrentEntries method*

```
private void getCurrentEntries() {

      // get all of the milestones for the project
      dataService.getEntries(new AsyncCallback<Vector<TimeEntryData>>() {

                   public void onFailure(Throwable caught) {
                         handleError(caught);
                   }

                   public void onSuccess(Vector<TimeEntryData> entries) {
                         int row = flexEntryTable.getRowCount();
                         for (TimeEntryData ted : entries) {
                               row++;
                               flexCurrentTable.setText(row, 0,
ted.getProject());
                               flexCurrentTable.setText(row, 1,
ted.getMilestone());
                               flexCurrentTable.setText(row, 2,
ted.getBillable() ? "Yes":"No");
                               flexCurrentTable.setText(row, 3,

                         DateTimeFormat.getShortDateFormat().format(ted.ge
                   tDate()));
                               flexCurrentTable.setText(row, 4,
                               String.valueOf(NumberFormat.getFormat(".00").form
                               at(ted.getHours())));
                               }
                   }
      });

}
```

You want to fetch the user's current entries at a couple of different points during the timecard process. First, after the user successfully logs in and is shown the UI, you want to fetch all of his current entries. Add the following code to the bottom of the loadMainUI method.

```
// get the current entries for the user
getCurrentEntries();
```

Second, after the user saves his timecard entries, you need to refresh the `FlexTable` to include the ones that he just entered. In the `onSuccess` Async method of the `saveEntries` method, add the following call.

```
// re-fetch the entries for the current user
getCurrentEntries();
```

Voilà! Your timecard application is now complete.

Summary

In this large and information-packed chapter you took a deep dive into the datastore and then used what you learned to complete your application. Since databases are an integral part of almost every application, it's worth recapping what you've learned.

Bigtable is a highly distributed and scalable service for storing and managing structured data. Bigtable is not a typical relational database that stores records as rows in a table. Instead, it stores data as entities with properties organized by application-defined kinds that can be manipulated using either low-level or high-level APIs.

Using JDO you can perform common CRUD operations as well as query for entities using JDOQL, a SQL-like query language. JDOQL supports filtering, sorting, and indexing of queries. At a high level, Bigtable supports transactions like most relational databases.

For the remainder of the chapter the focus was on finishing up your application. First you created an RPC data service that allowed your GWT front end to communicate with the server. You created quite a few classes and interfaces to implement this service as well as the objects that were passed between client and server layers. When you were done, you had a complete and working timecard application.

In the next chapter we'll focus on some of the functional services available to App Engine applications.a

CHAPTER 8

App Engine Services

In Chapter 7 you spent a lot of time in the data layer of the application stack. Let's take it up one level and focus on some of the functional services available to App Engine applications. The App Engine JRE has APIs for App Engine services that include a memory cache service, an HTTP request service, a mail API, an image API, and the Google Accounts API, which we discussed in Chapter 6. And, new to version 1.2.5, is the XMPP service, which allows your App Engine application to interact with XMPP-based applications like Google Talk.

This chapter starts with a quick review of the Memcache service, the URL Fetch service, and the Images service. We'll go a little deeper with some functional examples of the Mail API and the XMPP service. You'll be creating an application that sends an e-mail via the Mail API and also sends an instant message via XMPP.

Setting up the Project

Throughout this chapter you'll be using a single project for all the examples. To get that project started, create a new web application project in Eclipse. Call the project GAEJ – AppEngine Services. Make sure you uncheck Google Web Toolkit in the New Web Application Project dialog. Figure 8-1 shows the project settings I'll be using in the examples in this chapter.

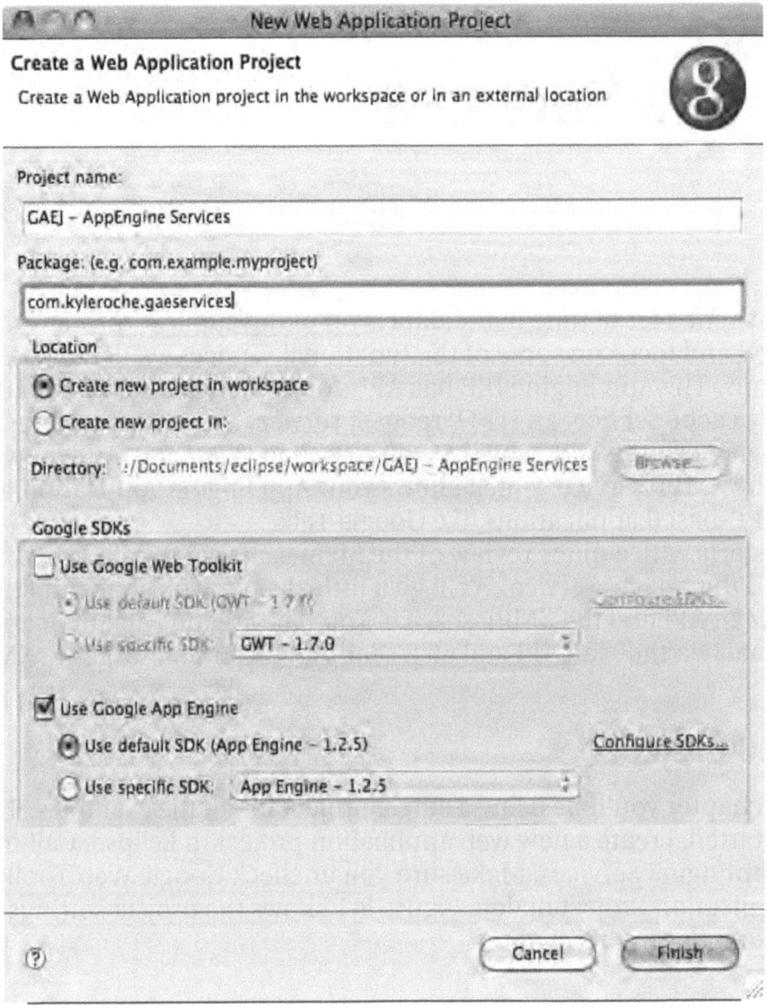

Figure 8-1. *New GAEJ project settings*

Now that you have created your project, you can get started with the Memcache service.

Memcache Service

App Engine provides a distributed in-memory data cache in front of the robust, persistent storage that you can use for certain transient tasks. The Memcache API supports the JCache interface. JCache is a draft standard that provides a map-like interface to the cached data store. Through JCache you store objects of any type or class in key/value pairs. This makes it very quick and simple to store and retrieve session data, query results, and subsets of data that will be reused throughout the application.

If you're running the same set of data-store queries multiple times in the same user's session, you should consider using the memory cache to speed the response time of the application. For example, consider a web site where users are browsing for a phonebook-type service in their area. If multiple users were all searching for Denver, CO, querying the data store on each request would become extremely inefficient. For queries with the same parameters, where the data is relatively static, you can store the results in the memory cache and have your query check there first. If the cache is expired or the results are no longer accessible, then the application can query the data store and refresh the cache with the new results. You can configure data to expire in two ways. You can provide an expiration time as a number of seconds relative to when the value is added, or as an absolute Unix epoch time in the future (for example, the number of seconds from midnight January 1, 1970).

No matter how you decide to approach expiration, there is one important design aspect to consider when using Memcache in your application. The data is not reliable, so make sure you store a copy of the data in the data store if the application requires the data to function properly. Data is not reliable because App Engine can expire the Memcache data at any time, even before the expiration deadline. That may make you a bit nervous, but don't worry too much. Memcache will try to keep the data for as long as possible. It will evict the data if the application is under pressure for memory resources, if you've coded the application to explicitly remove it, or if some sort of outage or restart has occurred. If you'd like to expire the data yourself, you have the option either to expire it after an amount of time has passed since the data has been set or at an absolute date and time. In all cases, your application should not assume that the data in the cache will be available.

Let's take a look at a sample application that uses the Memcache API to store data, retrieve data, and report usage statistics about the use of the cache. When you created the application for this chapter, the Google Plugin for Eclipse created some default files in the project. One of these is a servlet, which you'll be extending to exercise the Memcache API. Open the servlet in the src/com.kyleroche.gaeservices directory in your Eclipse project. Replace the default code with the code from Listing 8-1.

Listing 8-1. *Servlet code for the Memcache API example*

```java
package com.kyleroche.gaeservices;

import java.io.IOException;
import java.util.HashMap;
import java.util.Map;

import javax.cache.Cache;
import javax.cache.CacheException;
import javax.cache.CacheFactory;
import javax.cache.CacheManager;
import javax.cache.CacheStatistics;
import javax.servlet.http.*;

import com.google.appengine.api.memcache.MemcacheService;
import com.google.appengine.api.memcache.stdimpl.GCacheFactory;

@SuppressWarnings("serial")
public class GAEJ___AppEngine_ServicesServlet extends HttpServlet {
    public void doGet(HttpServletRequest req, HttpServletResponse resp)
                throws IOException {
          resp.setContentType("text/html");

          Cache cache = null;
          Map props = new HashMap();
          props.put(GCacheFactory.EXPIRATION_DELTA, 3600);
          props.put(MemcacheService.SetPolicy.ADD_ONLY_IF_NOT_PRESENT,
true);

          try {
              CacheFactory cacheFactory =
CacheManager.getInstance().getCacheFactory();
              cache = cacheFactory.createCache(props);
          } catch (CacheException e) {
              resp.getWriter().println(e.getMessage());
          }
```

```
        String key = "keyname";
        String value = "valuename";

        CacheStatistics stats = cache.getCacheStatistics();
        int hits = stats.getCacheHits();

        cache.put(key, value);
        resp.getWriter().println("<br />value is " +
cache.get(key).toString());
        resp.getWriter().println("<br />hit count is " + hits);


    }
}
```

Before you test the example, look at a few major sections of code in the preceding listing, Listing 8-1. The first thing you'll notice is that you have just about as many import statements as you do lines of code. There are no unused imports in the set. Listing 8-2 demonstrates how to query for the expiration of the cache.

Listing 8-2. *Cache configuration settings*

```
Map props = new HashMap();
props.put(GCacheFactory.EXPIRATION_DELTA, 3600);
props.put(MemcacheService.SetPolicy.ADD_ONLY_IF_NOT_PRESENT, true);

try {
        CacheFactory cacheFactory =
CacheManager.getInstance().getCacheFactory();
        cache = cacheFactory.createCache(props);
} catch (CacheException e) {
        resp.getWriter().println(e.getMessage());
}
```

In Listing 8-2 you can see where the GCacheFactory class is being used to set the expiration of the cache. As discussed earlier in this chapter, you can expire the cache after a specific period of time has passed or at an absolute date and time. In this case, you're using EXPIRATION_DELTA to set the cache to expire an hour after it's been set. The available configuration options that control expiration are listed in Table 8-1.

Table 8-1. *GCacheFactory expiration values*

Value	Description
EXPIRATION_DELTA	Expires after a relative number of seconds have passed
EXPIRATION_DELTA_MILLIS	Expires after a relative number of milliseconds have passed
EXPIRATION	Absolute date in time as a java.util.Date

As you move along in the code take note of where you set the key and value strings that you're putting in the cache. It's important to realize that you're not restricted to just Strings as objects in the cache. You can put any serializable object in the cache.

Take a look at the code in Listing 8-3. Here you are accessing the ConfigurationStatistics class to query some metrics on how many times your cache has been accessed, or hit.

Listing 8-3. *Cache statistics*

```
CacheStatistics stats = cache.getCacheStatistics();
int hits = stats.getCacheHits();
```

It's time to test out the application. Run it as a local web application. Since you're not using GWT, Eclipse will start a local web server and assign it a port. In most cases, unless you've reconfigured Eclipse, the address should be http://localhost:8080. Open the application. You should see something similar to Figure 8-2.

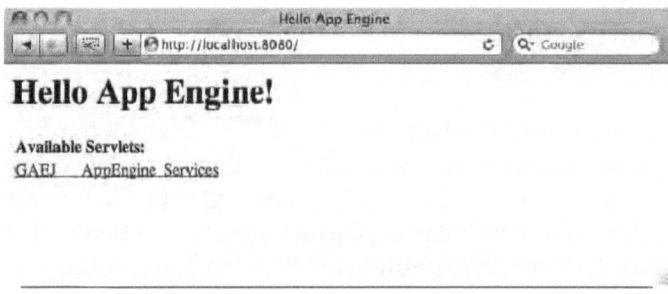

Figure 8-2. *Welcome page (index.html)*

Click the only listing in the Available Servlets list. This will open the servlet and run through your Memcache example, as shown in Figure 8-3.

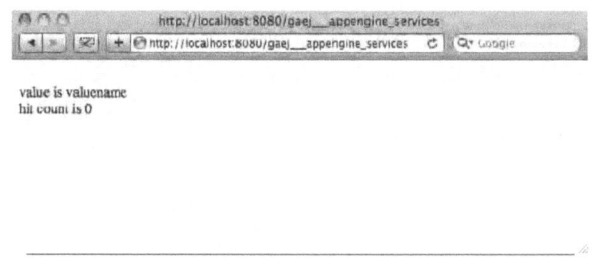

Figure 8-3. Cache example on first run

Take a look at the code again. Notice that you are pulling the cache statistics after you store your data and before you retrieve it from the cache. Because of this, the first time you access the application the hit count to your cache should be zero, as shown in Figure 8-3. Go ahead and reload the browser a few times and watch the hit count increase, as shown in Figure 8-4.

Figure 8-4. Thirteen refreshes later

That's Memcache. It was a short example, but you've learned how to configure your cache settings, store data, retrieve data, and query cache statistics in just 45 lines of code. Next we'll take a look at another App Engine service used for HTTP requests and responses.

URL Fetch Service

App Engine applications can communicate with other systems using HTTP and HTTPS callouts. This is a service that runs on the Google network infrastructure. It's fast and reliable. There are a few limitations, however. For example, an App Engine application can only access other resources on the web that are exposed over port 80 (HTTP) or port 443 (HTTPS). App Engine can't fetch URLs from non-standard ports or arbitrary port assignments. For the basic request-and-response scenario that we'll be looking at in this chapter, it doesn't make sense, but it's important to realize that your application is not actually communicating over a socket to the other systems on the web. As URLFetch is a service that runs on Google's infrastructure, your application is just invoking this service.

Consider the code in Listing 8-4. These two lines use the standard java.net namespace to fetch the response from a given URL. In this case, you're fetching the response from http://www.google.com. You are capturing the response by opening a stream to a new BufferedReader object. If you were to print this back to the screen, it would render what appears to be the Google landing pageGoogle landing page. However, by examining the URL in the browser's navigation bar, you will notice that you're still pointing to the App Engine application. See Figure 8-5 for an example of an App Engine application using URLFetch to retrieve the Google landing page.

Listing 8-4. *URL Fetch*

```
URL url = new URL("http://www.google.com/");
BufferedReader reader = new BufferedReader(new
InputStreamReader(url.openStream()));
```

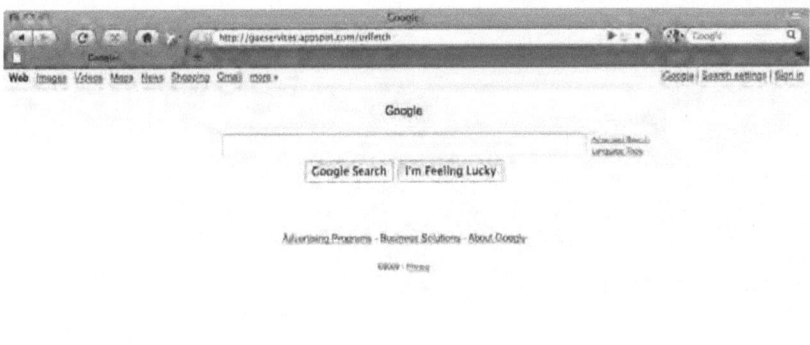

Figure 8-5. *Fetching google.com*

With that short example, you can start to conceptualize the potential scenarios for leveraging the URLFetch service. Using the URL Fetch service is how you address the creation of HTTP and HTTPS connections from App Engine. App Engine does not allow your application to make socket connections directly. You must use URL Fetch to achieve the same result. For example, take the scenario of a REST-based web service that your application would like to query. In any other JSP or Java environment, you could set up an HTTP connection to the web service's URI and parse the response directly. With App Engine, you must use URL Fetch to make the request, and then when your response is received, it's business as usual from there. For the full code used in the servlet that resulted in Figure 8-5, take a look at Listing 8-5.

Listing 8-5. *URL Fetch*

```
package com.kyleroche.gaeservices;

import java.io.BufferedReader;
import java.io.IOException;
import java.io.InputStreamReader;
import java.net.MalformedURLException;
import java.net.URL;

import javax.servlet.http.HttpServlet;
import javax.servlet.http.HttpServletRequest;
import javax.servlet.http.HttpServletResponse;

@SuppressWarnings("serial")
public class UrlFetchServlet extends HttpServlet{

        public void doGet(HttpServletRequest req, HttpServletResponse resp)
throws IOException {
                try {
                URL url = new URL("http://www.google.com");
                BufferedReader reader = new BufferedReader(new
InputStreamReader(url.openStream()));
                String line;

                while ((line = reader.readLine()) != null) {
                    resp.getOutputStream().println(line);
                }
                reader.close();
```

```
        } catch (MalformedURLException e) {
            resp.getOutputStream().println(e.getMessage());
        } catch (IOException e) {
            resp.getOutputStream().println(e.getMessage());
        }
    }
}
```

You can use URL Fetch to retrieve and parse XML documents, call RESTful web services, and read RSS feeds. If you want to look at a REST-based web service example, set the URL to http://ws.geonames.org/findNearby?lat=47.3&lng=9. This is an example of an XML-based web serviceXML-based web service that exposes a public REST API to return nearby country codes. Next, you'll take a quick look at another App Engine service for manipulating images.

Images Service

App Engine has a service, Images service, which can be leveraged for image manipulation. To demonstrate how to use this service, we'll walk you through the creation of a basic servlet that will flip uploaded images on the vertical axis. You'll continue to build on the same Eclipse project, but you need to add some more libraries:

1. This example uses the Apache Commons FileUpload package. Start by downloading that package from the following location: http://commons.apache.org/fileupload. We're using Version 1.2.1 for this example. Download and unzip the binary distribution of the package.

2. Drag the commons-fileupload-1.2.1.jar file from the lib directory into the WEB-INF/lib directory on the Eclipse Package ExplorerEclipse Package Explorer of your project.

3. Right-click the file in the Eclipse Package Explorer and select Build Path ➤ Add to Build Path.

4. You also need to use the Apache Commons IO library. Repeat the previous steps after downloading Commons IO from http://commons.apache.org/io. We're using version 1.4 for this example.

Creating the Java Classes

Now that the prerequisite libraries have been set up in your project, you'll need four new Java classes in order to leverage the Images service. Create a new servlet called `ImageTransform`. See Figure 8-6 for more information on the options you chose in the `New Java Class` dialog.

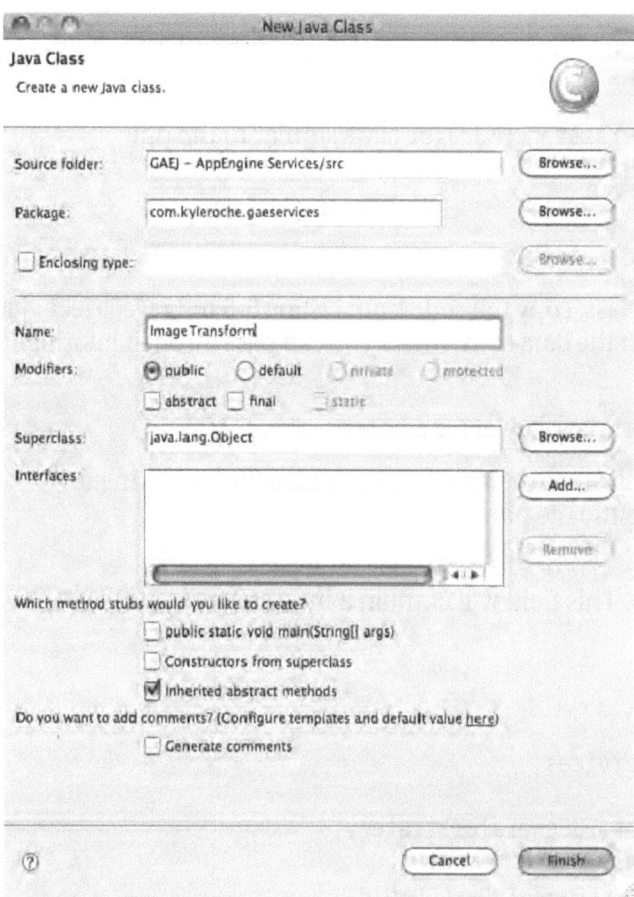

Figure 8-6. *Creating the ImageTransform servlet*

Repeat the previous step to create Java classes called ImageObject.java, ImageSource.java, and PMF.java. Each of these has a specific purpose in the application:

- The ImageObject class defines the attributes that you'll store for each image you upload in the App Engine data store.

- The ImageSource servlet renders your images back to the browser after retrieving them from the data store.

- The ImageTransform servlet does the processing of the POST request and stores the files in the data store.

- The PMF class is a PersistanceManager class similar to the one discussed in Chapter 7.

Writing the ImageObject Class

Starting with the ImageObject class, copy the code from Listing 8-6 to ImageObject.java. This code defines three fields in the data store where you can pass through information about your image requests.

- The first, *id*, is the primary key of type Long.

- The second, *name*, will store the name of the image file in a string. In this case, this will be the file name.

- The third, *ImageObject*, is of type com.google.appengine. api.datastore.Blob. This field will contain a byte array of your image's source file.

Listing 8-6. *ImageObject.java*

```
package com.kyleroche.gaeservices;
import java.util.Date;
import javax.jdo.annotations.IdGeneratorStrategy;
import javax.jdo.annotations.IdentityType;
import javax.jdo.annotations.PersistenceCapable;
import javax.jdo.annotations.Persistent;
import javax.jdo.annotations.PrimaryKey;

@PersistenceCapable(identityType = IdentityType.APPLICATION)
public class ImageObject {
    @PrimaryKey
```

```java
@Persistent(valueStrategy = IdGeneratorStrategy.IDENTITY)
private Long id;

@Persistent
private String name;

@Persistent
private com.google.appengine.api.datastore.Blob content;

@Persistent
private Date date;

public ImageObject(String name, com.google.appengine.api.datastore.Blob
content, Date date) {
    this.name = name;
    this.content = content;
    this.date = date;
}

public Long getId() {
    return id;
}

public String getName() {
    return name;
}

public com.google.appengine.api.datastore.Blob getContent() {
    return content;
}

public Date getDate() {
    return date;
}

public void setName(String name) {
    this.name = name;
}
```

```
    public void setContent(com.google.appengine.api.datastore.Blob content)
{
        this.content = content;
    }

    public void setDate(Date date) {
        this.date = date;
    }
}
```

Writing the PersistenceManagerFactory Class

Now that you've defined the data structure where you'll be storing your images, you can build the PersistenceManagerFactory class, like you did in Chapter 7, to facilitate communication with the data store. Copy the code from Listing 8-7 into PMF.java.

Listing 8-7. *PMF.java*

```
package com.kyleroche.gaeservices;
import javax.jdo.JDOHelper;
import javax.jdo.PersistenceManagerFactory;

public final class PMF {
    private static final PersistenceManagerFactory pmfInstance =
        JDOHelper.getPersistenceManagerFactory("transactions-optional");

    private PMF() {}

    public static PersistenceManagerFactory get() {
        return pmfInstance;
    }
}
```

Writing the ImageSource Class

There are two more new classes to create, and then you'll set up the HTML form to upload your image file for transformation. The ImageSource.java file retrieves the byte array you stored in the data store and renders it back to the browser. It uses an HTML parameter named "id" to filter the data-store query. Actually, to be accurate, you're using the getObjectById method of the PersistenceManager class to retrieve the image object. Copy the code from Listing 8-8 to the ImageSource servlet you already created.

Listing 8-8. ImageSource.java

```java
package com.kyleroche.gaeservices;

import java.io.IOException;
import javax.jdo.PersistenceManager;
import javax.servlet.http.HttpServlet;
import javax.servlet.http.HttpServletRequest;
import javax.servlet.http.HttpServletResponse;

@SuppressWarnings("serial")
public class ImageSource extends HttpServlet{

        public void doGet(HttpServletRequest req, HttpServletResponse resp)
throws IOException {
                resp.setContentType("image/jpeg");
                PersistenceManager pm = PMF.get().getPersistenceManager();


        resp.getOutputStream().write(pm.getObjectById(ImageObject.class,
Long.valueOf(req.getParameter("id").toString()))).getContent().getBytes());
                resp.getOutputStream().flush();
                resp.getOutputStream().close();
        }
}
```

Writing the ImageTransform Class

So far, you've created the `PersistenceManager` class to handle the communication with the data store, the `ImageObject` itself, and the servlet to retrieve and render the image from the data store. The next piece is the most significant. How do you handle the HTTP POST form that will be sending you the image and apply the transformation prior to storing the image in the data store? The `ImageTransform` servlet that you first added to your project is going to accept the POST parameters from the HTML form, save the image to the data store, call the App Engine Images service to transform the image, and display both the original and the transformed images to the browser.

Copy the code from Listing 8-9 to `ImageTransform.java`. Pay close attention to the line of code in bold print. This is where the transformation is defined. You are telling the Images service what type of transformation you are going to apply to the image before you commit the changes.

Listing 8-9. ImageTransform.java

```java
package com.kyleroche.gaeservices;

import java.io.BufferedInputStream;
import java.io.InputStream;
import java.io.PrintWriter;
import java.util.Date;

import javax.jdo.PersistenceManager;
import javax.servlet.http.HttpServlet;
import javax.servlet.http.HttpServletRequest;
import javax.servlet.http.HttpServletResponse;

import org.apache.commons.fileupload.FileItemIterator;
import org.apache.commons.fileupload.FileItemStream;
import org.apache.commons.fileupload.servlet.ServletFileUpload;
import org.apache.commons.io.IOUtils;

import com.google.appengine.api.images.Image;
import com.google.appengine.api.images.ImagesService;
import com.google.appengine.api.images.ImagesServiceFactory;
import com.google.appengine.api.images.Transform;

@SuppressWarnings("serial")
public class ImageTransform extends HttpServlet{
    public void doGet(HttpServletRequest req, HttpServletResponse resp)
    {
        doPost(req, resp);
    }

    public void doPost(HttpServletRequest req, HttpServletResponse resp)
{
        ServletFileUpload upload = new ServletFileUpload();
        upload.setSizeMax(50000000);

        PrintWriter pw = null;
        try {
            resp.reset();
            pw = resp.getWriter();
            resp.setContentType("text/html");

            FileItemIterator iterator = upload.getItemIterator(req);
```

```
                        while (iterator.hasNext()) {
                                FileItemStream item = iterator.next();
                                InputStream in = item.openStream();

                                BufferedInputStream bis = new
BufferedInputStream(in);
                                byte[] bisArray = IOUtils.toByteArray(bis);

                                Date date = new Date();

                                ImagesService imagesService =
ImagesServiceFactory.getImagesService();

                                Image origImage =
ImagesServiceFactory.makeImage(bisArray);
                                        com.google.appengine.api.datastore.Blob origBlob
= new com.google.appengine.api.datastore.Blob(origImage.getImageData());
                                        ImageObject origImageObject = new
ImageObject("origFile.jpg", origBlob, date);

                                Transform flip =
ImagesServiceFactory.makeHorizontalFlip();
                                Image newImage =
imagesService.applyTransform(flip, origImage);
                                        com.google.appengine.api.datastore.Blob newBlob =
new com.google.appengine.api.datastore.Blob(newImage.getImageData());
                                        ImageObject newImageObject = new
ImageObject("newFile.jpg", newBlob, date);

                                PersistenceManager pm =
PMF.get().getPersistenceManager();

                                try {
                                        pm.makePersistent(origImageObject);
                                        pm.makePersistent(newImageObject);

                                        pw.println("<HTML><HEAD></HEAD><BODY>");
                                        pw.println("<img src='" + "/ImageSource" +
"?id=" + String.valueOf(origImageObject.getId()) + "'/>");
                                        pw.println("<img src='" + "/ImageSource" +
"?id=" + String.valueOf(newImageObject.getId()) + "'/>");
                                        pw.println("</BODY></HTML>");
                                } catch (Exception ex) {
                                        // do something
```

```
                    }
                }
            } catch (Exception ex) {
                //do something
            }
        }
    }
}
```

Completing the Application

There are just a few more steps to finish before you can test this example. First, you need to adjust the index.html file that was created with your App Engine project. You're going to add a basic HTML form to POST your uploaded image to the ImageTransform servlet you created. Copy the code from Listing 8-10 to war/WEB-INF/index.html. Paste the code block just before the closing BODY tag.

Listing 8-10. war/WEB-INF/index.html

```html
<form action="ImageTransform" method="POST" enctype="multipart/form-data">
    <div id="status" style="text-align:center;color:red"></div>
    <table align="center">
      <tr>
        <td colspan="2" style="font-weight:bold;">Please select your file
to upload:</td>
      </tr>
      <tr>
        <td>File:</td>
        <td><input type="file" name="fileObj"/></td>
      </tr>
      <tr>
       <td colspan="2" align="center">
         <input type="submit"/>
       </td>
      </tr>
    </table>
   </form>
```

Finally, you need to map your new servlet so App Engine knows where to send your POST request. Open the web.xml file in the war/WEB-INF/lib directory of the App Engine project and add the code from Listing 8-11. The XML elements in Listing 8-11 map the ImageTransform and ImageSource servlets to their respective URL patterns.

Listing 8-11. *Add to war/WEB-INF/lib/web.xml*

```
<servlet>
        <servlet-name>ImageTransform</servlet-name>
        <servlet-class>com.kyleroche.gaeservices.ImageTransform</servlet-
class>
</servlet>
<servlet>
        <servlet-name>ImageSource</servlet-name>
        <servlet-class>com.kyleroche.gaeservices.ImageSource</servlet-class>
</servlet>
<servlet-mapping>
        <servlet-name>ImageTransform</servlet-name>
        <url-pattern>/ImageTransform</url-pattern>
</servlet-mapping>
<servlet-mapping>
        <servlet-name>ImageSource</servlet-name>
        <url-pattern>/ImageSource</url-pattern>
</servlet-mapping>
```

Testing the Service

You're ready to test the service. Locate a jpg file you can use for testing. In this example, we're using the image of the book cover. Start the application by choosing Run As ➤ Web Application from the Run menu in Eclipse. The application will start up and display the path in the Eclipse console, as shown in Figure 8-7.

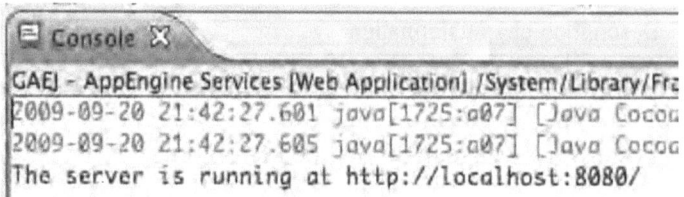

Figure 8-7. *Path to the application shown in the Eclipse console (Mac OS X)*

Open your browser to the URL shown in your Eclipse console. Click the Browse button to select a file to upload. Navigate to the JPG image you selected earlier, select that image, and then click Submit. The result of the upload is shown in Figure 8-8 where the book cover is rendered along with a mirror image flipped on the vertical axis.

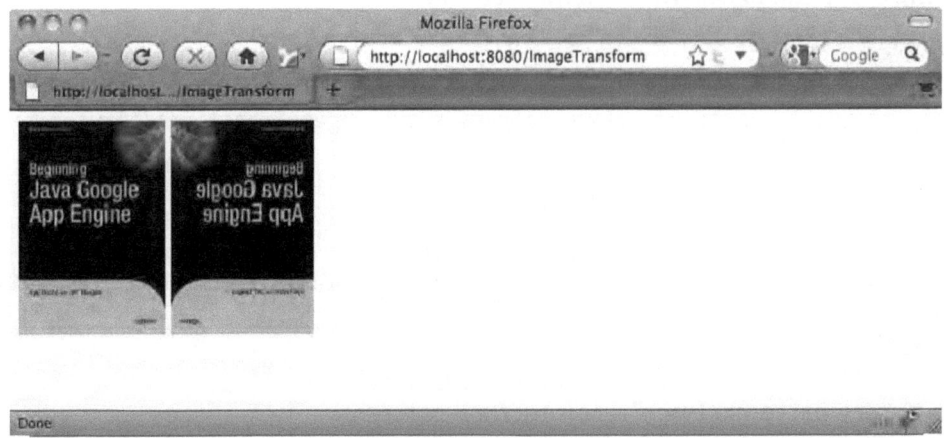

Figure 8-8. *Transformed book cover*

In this section you used the Images service in Google App Engine to flip an uploaded image on its vertical axis. You also leveraged some of the things you learned about the data store in Chapter 7. Before moving on to the Mail API, experiment with the transformation options available from the Images service. You can find a full list of available transformations and their descriptions in Table 8-1.

Table 8-1. *Image transformations*

Transformation	Description of Transformation
Resize	Resizes images while maintaining the same aspect ratio
Rotate	Rotates the image in 90-degree increments
Flip Horizontally	Flips the image on the horizontal axis
Flip Vertically	Flips the image on the vertical axis
Crop	Crops the image using a bounding box
I'm feeling Lucky	Auto-adjusts the image to enhance dark and bright colors to optimal levels

Next, you're going to use two services to interact with users outside of your application.

Mail API

The services we've looked at so far this chapter have all been background-processing or behind-the-scenes services. It's time to take a look at a few services that let you interact with the world outside of your application. Starting with App Engine's Mail API, Google App Engine Mail service supports the JavaMail interface for sending e-mails programmatically from within an application. Your application can send e-mails on behalf of either the application administrator or the currently logged-in user. To see a full list of features, reference the JavaMail API by visiting http://java.sun.com/products/javamail/javadocs/index.html. The App Engine Mail API implements the full JavaMail API excluding the ability to connect to other mail services for sending and receiving e-mail messages. Any SMTP configuration added to the Transport or Session will be ignored.

As mentioned, the Mail service Java API supports the JavaMail interface. This means that you have the ability to add e-mail targets to blind copy e-mail addresses, send HTML-formatted messages, and add multiple attachments. There's no need to provide any SMTP server configuration when you create a JavaMail session. App Engine will always use the Mail service for sending messages, which can be distributed to individuals or to large distribution lists. Messages count against your application quota (see Chapter 3 for more details), but you get plenty of transactions per day to fit almost any use case. You can also send attachments using the Mail service. There are limitations on the size of attachments you can send along with a message. Reference the online documentation for the current size limits. Table 8-2 shows a list of accepted MIME types and their corresponding file-name extensions.

Table 8-2. MIME Types accepted by the Mail service

MIME Type	Filename Extension
image/x-ms-bmp	bmp
text/css	css
text/comma-separated-values	csv
image/gif	gif

MIME Type	Filename Extension
text/html	htm html
image/jpeg	jpeg jpg jpe
application/pdf	pdf
image/png	png
application/rss+sml	rss
text/plain	text txt asc diff pot
image/tiff	tiff tif
image/vnd.wap.wbmp	wbmp
text/calendar	ics
text/x-vcard	vcf

The Mail service works only on deployed App Engine applications. The code in Listing 8-12, which you'll be using in this demonstration, will not send an e-mail running locally on the development server. You're going to use the same Eclipse project you used for the previous examples in this chapter. Create a new Java class called MailServlet.java. Copy the code from Listing 8-12 to the new servlet.

Listing 8-12. *MailServlet.java*

```
package com.kyleroche.gaeservices;

import java.io.IOException;
import java.util.Properties;

import javax.mail.Message;
import javax.mail.MessagingException;
import javax.mail.Session;
import javax.mail.Transport;
import javax.mail.internet.AddressException;
import javax.mail.internet.InternetAddress;
import javax.mail.internet.MimeMessage;
```

```java
import javax.servlet.http.*;

@SuppressWarnings("serial")
public class MailServlet extends HttpServlet{
    public void doGet(HttpServletRequest req, HttpServletResponse resp)
    throws IOException {
        resp.setContentType("text/html");

        Properties props = new Properties();
        Session session = Session.getDefaultInstance(props, null);

        String messageBody = "What do you think about the book. You
can reply to this and I'll get it.";

        try {
            Message emailMessage = new MimeMessage(session);
            emailMessage.setFrom(new
InternetAddress("kyle.m.roche@gmail.com", "The Author"));
            emailMessage.addRecipient(Message.RecipientType.TO, new
InternetAddress("", "The Reader"));
            emailMessage.setSubject("How's the book?");
            emailMessage.setText(messageBody);
            Transport.send(emailMessage);
            resp.getOutputStream().println("Message sent!");
        } catch (AddressException e) {

        } catch (MessagingException e) {

        }
    }
}
```

Let's review the code before you deploy and test the application. The application's entire logic lives in the doGet method of the servlet's class. This means that all the code will execute as soon as a user browses to this page of the application. Inside the try/catch block you are creating a new instance of the Message class, and then passing it to the Transport.send method to initiate the sending of the message. Since, at the time of this writing, Google restricts each user to only 10 deployed applications on App Engine, you might not want to create a new application ID and deploy this example. However, you can always reuse an application ID from a previous chapter to test out the Mail service in a deployed application. Figure 8-9 shows the e-mail message sent from a deployed copy of this servlet.

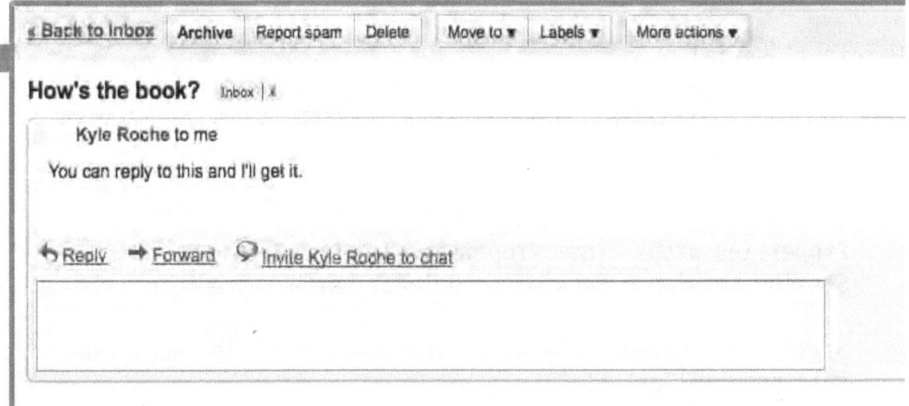

Figure 8-9. Email sent from the App Engine Mail service

In this section you viewed the features of App Engine's Mail service. You learned that only deployed applications can use the Mail service. Once deployed, you can send e-mails to individuals or larger distribution groups. Sometimes Mail isn't the best option for communicating with your application's users. What if you had a requirement for using instant messaging? Well, Google App Engine provides an XMPP service in addition to the other services discussed in this chapter.

XMPP Service

The XMPP service works slightly differently from the Mail service in that users must perform an action before you can send them a message. With the Mail API, you only had to worry about valid "from" addresses. You could send a message to whomever you wanted. With XMPP, users to whom you are going to send a message need to add the App Engine application to their Google Talk friend list or their Jabber client buddy list. In this example, you'll use Google Talk. If you don't have a Google Talk account, you can register for a free account at https://www.google.com/accounts/NewAccount?service=talk.

This example requires that you deploy this application to App Engine. The XMPP service will not work from the local development server. This example uses the App Engine application ID apressxmpp. If you recall from Chapter 3, application IDs are unique across all App Engine applications. Once deployed, your application gets its own appspot.com domain name. In addition, the applications also get a mapped handler in the form of an e-mail address, for example, apressxmpp@appspot.com. Before you can have your application send you an instant message you need to add the application to your friend list in Google Talk. In the web interface for Google Talk, which is nested inside the Gmail interface, we've added apressxmpp@appspot.com as illustrated in Figure 8-10.

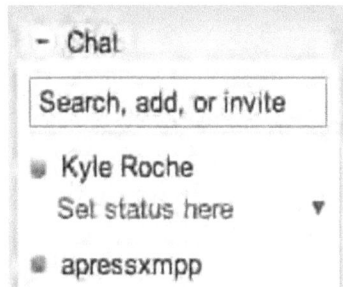

Figure 8-10. Application ID added to Google Talk

You can see that the application appears to be online. You can send it messages, but it will not respond. You're just going to be looking at sending XMPP messages. If you'd like to enable your application to receive XMPP messages, reference the online documentation at http://code.google.com/appengine. Create a servlet called XMPPServlet.java in the same Eclipse project that you've been using throughout this chapter. Copy the code from Listing 8-13 into the new servlet.

Listing 8-13. MailServlet.java

```
package com.kyleroche.xmpp;

import java.io.IOException;
import javax.servlet.http.*;
import com.google.appengine.api.xmpp.JID;
import com.google.appengine.api.xmpp.Message;
import com.google.appengine.api.xmpp.MessageBuilder;
import com.google.appengine.api.xmpp.SendResponse;
import com.google.appengine.api.xmpp.XMPPService;
import com.google.appengine.api.xmpp.XMPPServiceFactory;

@SuppressWarnings("serial")
public class XMPPServlet extends HttpServlet {
    public void doGet(HttpServletRequest req, HttpServletResponse resp)
                throws IOException {
        JID jid = new JID("put your gmail account here");
```

```
            String msgBody = "App Engine is pretty cool. I can't believe it's
this easy to send XMPP!";
        Message msg = new MessageBuilder()
            .withRecipientJids(jid)
            .withBody(msgBody)
            .build();

        boolean messageSent = false;
        XMPPService xmpp = XMPPServiceFactory.getXMPPService();
        if (xmpp.getPresence(jid).isAvailable()) {
            SendResponse status = xmpp.sendMessage(msg);
            messageSent = (status.getStatusMap().get(jid) ==
SendResponse.Status.SUCCESS);
        }

        if (!messageSent) {
            // do something
        }
    }
}
```

There's not much to it. You're creating an instance of the XMPPService and using the com.google.appengine.api.xmpp.JID class to define the Jabber ID that will be receiving your message. Save this servlet after putting your own Gmail ID in place of *put your gmail account here*. Deploy the project to App Engine. Don't forget to map your servlet in your web.xml file. Once you land on the page, if you've already added the application to your friend list, you should get an instant message right away. An example message is displayed in Figure 8-10.

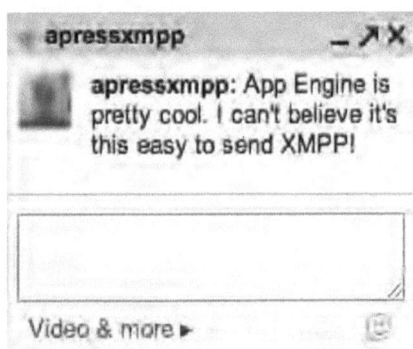

Figure 8-10. *XMPP Message received from App Engine*

The XMPP service is another great way to enable your application to reach out to your user base in more creative ways. Traditional e-mail is available in almost every consumer application. Google provides a simple, easy-to-use XMPP service that allows you to create cutting-edge applications that can actually instant message application users!

Summary

In this chapter you took a tour of the services that App Engine provides. First, you reviewed the Memcache service, which allows you to cache data to keep from making roundtrips to the data store and to maximize the speed of your application. Next, you tried out the URLFetch service. URLFetch can be used to interact with RESTful APIs, send POST data, and get HTTP responses. Finally, you constructed a brief demonstration that pulls the HTML response from www.google.com using a GET request.

The other three services were a bit more advanced. You built a servlet to accept an uploaded image file, which you stored in the App Engine data store. You then took this image and transformed it using the App Engine Images service. You flipped the image on the vertical axis and rendered both the original and the altered versions back to the user. Finally, you got a brief look at two App Engine services that allow you to interact with users outside of your application. The Mail API can be used to send messages to individuals or distribution lists. You built a servlet that sends an e-mail with a simple message to a hard-coded user. Then you took that a step further and sent a user an instant message using the XMPP service that App Engine provides. All these services increase the value of building your application on Google App Engine. Having these services available to you in such an easy fashion makes you wonder why you'd ever need to build an application stack from the bottom up again. In Chapter 9 we're going to take a look at some more advanced scenarios using Google App Engine.

CHAPTER 9

■■■

Administration and Integration

You started out by creating your first App Engine application and finished with a pretty complicated example application, and you got a tour of the major features of Google App Engine. In this final section we're going to introduce you to some of the more advanced aspects of App Engine . You'll learn how to maintain and monitor your application once it's been deployed to appspot.com, and you'll try out some new and exciting approaches to integration.

Nearly every application you write needs to integrate with another system. It's rare that you can encapsulate all your application needs in your code. In most cases you're going to have to connect to a financial system, an ERP system, a warehouse management system, or a number of other technology components. Since you're considering App Engine for your application's platform, you've already considered the benefits and value statements around cloud computing. It's common for cloud-computing application platforms to connect to other cloud-computing platforms. For example, you may be writing a business application on App Engine that needs to retrieve information from Salesforce.com, a CRM system. In this chapter, we'll walk you through some integration scenarios, and we'll introduce you to some cutting-edge technologies that are also cloud-based.

Managing Your App Engine Application

After you have deployed your application, you can use Google's Administration Console for App Engine to manage, monitor, and configure your application. From the Administration Console you can create new Application IDs, invite other developers to contribute to your application, view access data and error logs, analyze traffic, browse the datastore, manage your scheduled tasks, and much more. This is the central location for managing and monitoring your App Engine application.

The App Engine Administration Console comes in two flavors. If you've been using your personal Google account, you can simply log in to `http://appengine.google.com` to manage your applications. If you're using a Google Apps account to develop on App Engine, you should use the Administration Console located at http://appengine.google.com/a/yourdomain.com, where *yourdomain.com* is your Google Apps domain name. It's important to note that since some services aren't yet available on Google Apps (Reader, Blogger, Google Voice) many people have logins that match their Google Apps domain for the public services. If this is the case, your App Engine applications will show up only in your Google Apps Administration Console. Your list will appear empty until you log in with the /a/yourdomain.com suffix.

Start by logging in to the appropriate URI to open your Google Apps Administration Console. Reference Table 9-1 for the correct URI. You might be prompted for your Google Accounts credentials.

Table 9-1. *App Engine Administration Consoles*

Google Account Type	Administration Console URL
Google Apps (@yourdomain.com)	http://appengine.google.com/a/yourdomain.com
Google Accounts (@gmail.com or @other.com)	http://appengine.google.com

Once you've logged in you should see the list of applications you've created so far. You'll see two columns, as shown in Figure 9-1.

My Applications

Application	Current Version
apresswave	1
apressxmpp	1

Figure 9-1. *The My Applications list*

The Application column shows the App Engine application ID. This is the same name you used when you deployed your application to appspot.com. Each registered application gets a unique subdomain under appspot.com. Because of this and to prevent domain-name parking, you are restricted to a total of 10 registered applications. There's no way to rename or delete applications at this time, so choose your names carefully!

The Current Version column lists the App Engine version for each of your applications. You can click the link to see the running application. Each unique version you deploy to App Engine gets its own URI, so you can test your changes before rolling them out. Each application version you upload can be accessed

directly through the version's unique URI, which is formatted as follows:
http://*version*.latest.*applicationID*.appspot.com, where *version* is the unique
version number version number (for example, 1, 2, 3,), and *applicationID* is
the application identifier for App Engine. Each application can have one default
application version. We'll show you how to set the default version and list the other
uploaded versions later in this chapter. Click any of the application names in the
left column of your My Applications page. This will open the dashboard for that
application. Let's take a deeper look at some of the features of the dashboard.

The Application Dashboard

When you open the dashboard for one of your App Engine applications you get a
snapshot of the key metrics of the running application. Take a look at Figure 9-2. You
should see something similar on your application's dashboard.

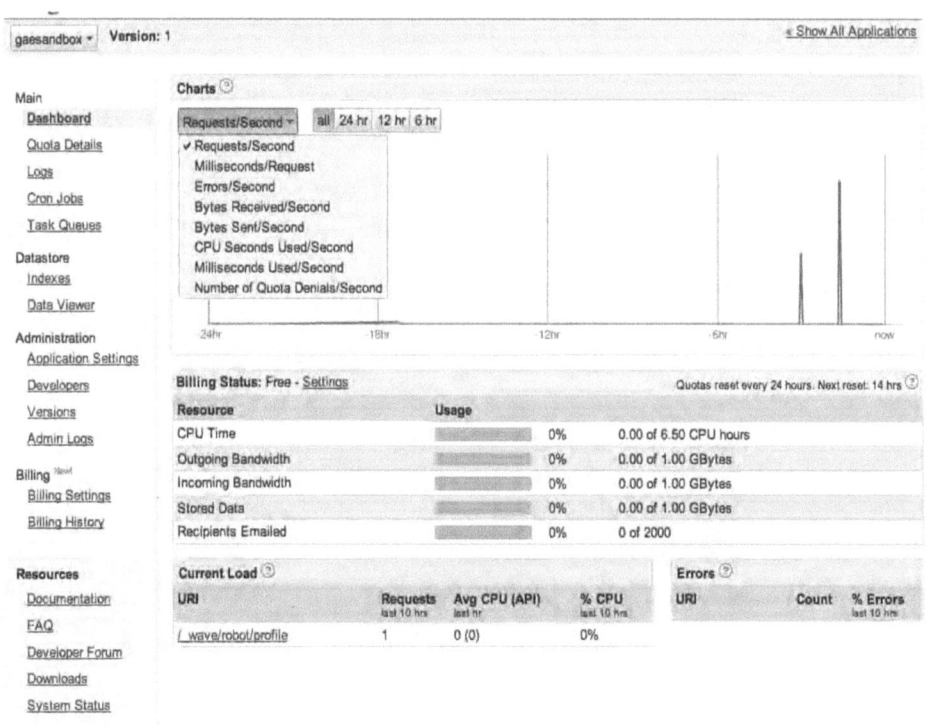

Figure 9-2. *The application dashboard*

Three components make up the header of the dashboard. They are the navigation utility to switch to another App Engine application's dashboard, the version selector, and the link back to your application list. Keep in mind that multiple versions of the same application can be live simultaneously. Let's walk through the navigation links in the left column and take a look at what each of these do in more detail.

Table 9-2. *App Engine Administration Consoles*

Administration Console	Purpose
Dashboard	The dashboard (Figure 9-3) displays high-level information about the running application, its versions, traffic, and quotas.

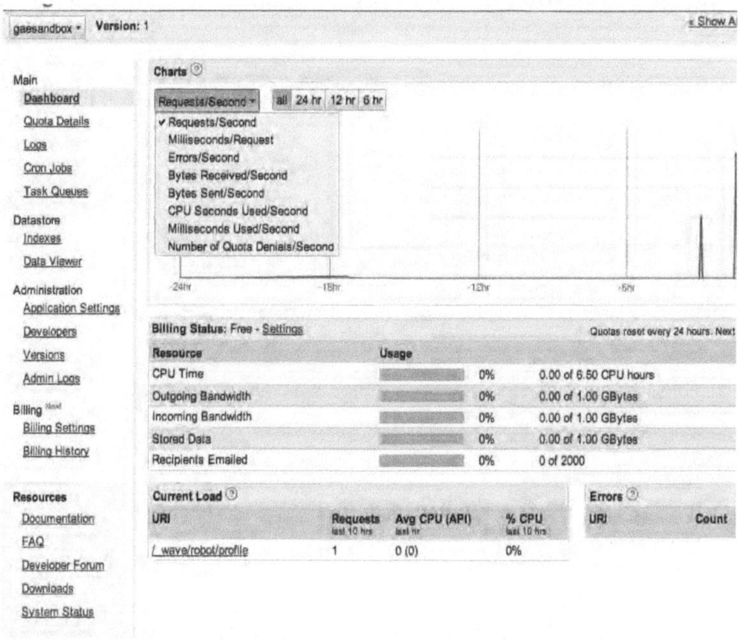

Figure 9-3. *The dashboard*

Administration Console	Purpose
Quota Details	The Quota Details utility (Figure 9-4) shows all the quotas and where your application stands in relation to your limits.

The quota details for this application are grouped by API and are listed below. If your application exceeds 50% of any particular quota halfway through the day, it may exceed the quota before the day is over. To learn more about how quotas work, read Understanding Quotas and Why Is My App Over Quota?

Requests
Quotas are reset every 24 hours. Next reset: 9 hours

Resource	Daily Quota			Rate
CPU Time		0%	0.00 of 6.50 CPU hours	Okay
Requests		0%	5 of 1333328	Okay
Outgoing Bandwidth		0%	0.00 of 1.00 GBytes	Okay
Incoming Bandwidth		0%	0.00 of 1.00 GBytes	Okay
Secure Requests		0%	0 of 1333328	Okay
Secure Outgoing Bandwidth		0%	0.00 of 1.00 GBytes	Okay
Secure Incoming Bandwidth		0%	0.00 of 1.00 GBytes	Okay

Datastore

Datastore API Calls		0%	0 of 10368000	Okay
Stored Data		0%	0.00 of 1.00 GBytes	Okay
Data Sent to API		0%	0.00 of 12.00 GBytes	Okay
Data Received from API		0%	0.00 of 116.00 GBytes	Okay
Datastore CPU Time		0%	0.00 of 62.11 CPU hours	Okay

Mail

Mail API Calls		0%	0 of 7000	Okay
Recipients Emailed		0%	0 of 2000	Okay
Admins Emailed		0%	0 of 5000	Okay
Message Body Data Sent		0%	0.00 of 0.06 GBytes	Okay
Attachments Sent		0%	0 of 2000	Okay
Attachment Data Sent		0%	0.00 of 0.10 GBytes	Okay

Figure 9-4. *The Quota Details utility*

Logs	Use the App Engine Logs utility (Figure 9-5) to debug your application using five levels of sensitivity. From Debug, the least severe, to Critical, the most severe, you can see any recent error messages from your application.

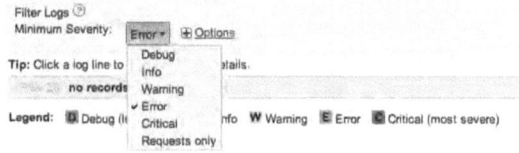

Figure 9-5. *The Logs utility*

Administration Console	Purpose
Cron Jobs	You can schedule cron jobs within the `cron.xml` file in the project's `WEB-INF` folder. This view will be empty until you create a cron job.
Task Queues	Task queues allow you to run code outside of a user request. If an application needs to execute some background work, it may use the Task Queue API. You can manage your task queues from this console.
Indexes	Datastore indexes are defined in the `datastore-indexes.xml` configuration file for each application. Refer to Chapter 7 for more details on datastore indexes.
Data Viewer	You can query data in the datastore directly from this view using Google Query Language (GQL).).
Application Settings	In the application settings view you can set the Applications Title, the Authentication Options, Cookie Expiration, and you can manage inbound services like XMPP.
Developers	Invite other developers to contribute to the application.
Versions	Manage the different versions you've deployed, and set the default version for the application. Figure 9-6 shows an example of an application with three deployed versions, where version 2 is the default version.

Figure 9-6. *Multiple versions of an application*

Admin Logs	The Admin log displays actions committed by application administrators using the Administration Console or the SDK.

Administration Console	Purpose
Billing Settings	You can enable billing on your App Engine application and set higher application quotas through the Billing Settings view. If you've already enabled billing, you can set your Billing Administrator here as well as manage your Resource Allocations and Daily Budgets.
Billing History	You can access your usage reports and billing events in the Billing History view.

Application Versioning

Now that you know your way around the Administration Console, it's time to dive a bit deeper into versioning your applications. In Chapter 3 you deployed your first App Engine application using the Deployment utility that came with the Google Plugin forGoogle Plugin for Eclipse. From the deployment configuration dialog, shown in Figure 9-7, you have the opportunity to set the version number. Open one of your previous projects from this book and click the App Engine icon in the toolbar to open the deployment configuration dialog. Click App Engine project settings to open the dialog shown in Figure 9-7.

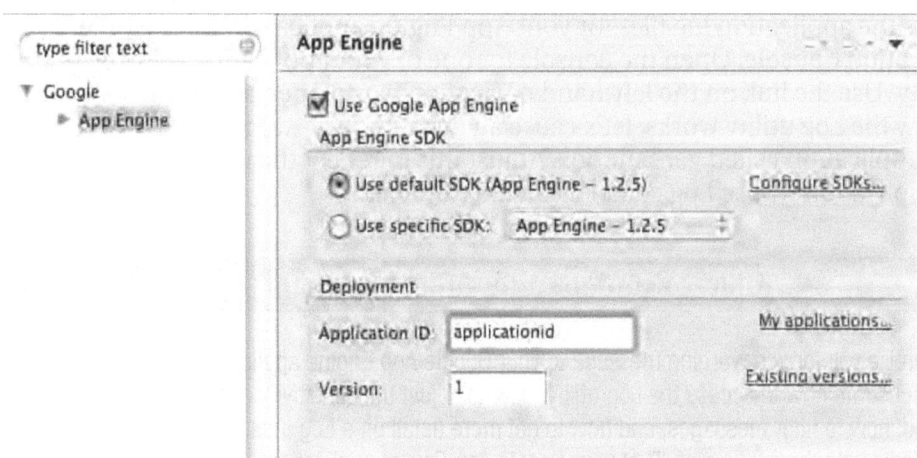

Figure 9-7. The deployment configuration dialog

This dialog changes the value in the war/WEB-INF/lib/appengine-config.xml file before the application is deployed. This file holds the same configuration data that you can configure in the deployment configuration utility. Listing 9-1 contains a sample portion of the appengine-config.xml file.

Listing 9-1. *appengine-config.xml*

```
<?xml version="1.0" encoding="utf-8"?>
<appengine-web-app xmlns="http://appengine.google.com/ns/1.0">
<application>applicationid</application>
<version>1</version>
```

Go ahead and set the application's version to 2. You can do this by either changing the value in the appengine-config.xml file or through the App Engine application settings dialog of the deployment configuration utility. Once you've redeployed your application to App Engine, you'll see that both versions are available in the Versions section of your Administration Console (see Figure 9-6). You'll notice that the new version is not automatically set as the default version. You must manually set the default version in the Administration Console.

Analyzing Log Files

Often your application runs perfectly both locally and in debug mode, but when you deploy it, something unexpected happens. As mentioned earlier in this chapter, you can access the application log files for your App Engine application through the Administration Console. Open the console for one of your applications. Switch to the Logs utility. Use the link on the left-hand navigation bar to open the application's log. To see how the Log utility works, let's cause an error. In this example case, we're using an application called gaesandbox. Adjust this to reflect the name of the App Engine application whose Log console you have opened.

Analyze Google App Engine Log Files

This exercise will force a warning message to your Google App Engine application's log file. It will demonstrate how to access the Log utility, how to adjust the sensitivity of the messages displayed, how to filter messages, and how to get more detail on a Log message. Replace applicationid with the application ID of your Google App Engine application.

1. Open your browser to http://applicationid.appspot.com/ thispathdoesnotexist.

2. You'll receive an HTTP 404 error message.

3. Open your App Engine Administration Console. Click the Logs link in the left navigation panel.

4. Change the Minimum Severity to Debug.

5. Open the most recent Warning message by clicking the plus (+) sign to the left of the message. The subject should be No handlers matched this URL.

6. Analyze the message. You'll notice that the URL that you tried to access in the first step is what caused this warning in the application. For example, if this were a real situation you might have inadvertently excluded an entry in your web.xml file.

7. Expand the Options link to the right of the Minimum Severity drop-down. In the Filter text field enter **URL**, and then click View. Experiment with the other options to show messages before or after certain time periods.

This was a quick example of how to analyze the Google App Engine application log for warning messages. In this case you caused a 404 Not Found error by attempting to access an invalid path.

Downloading Log Files

You can download the log files from your application for more detailed analysis. To download the logs to your local computer, use the request_logs action of your appcfg utility, which came with the App Engine SDK. Listing 9-2 shows the command syntax for Mac OS X. Listing 9-3 shows the command syntax for Windows.

Listing 9-2. *Download log files on Mac OS X*

```
appengine-java-sdk/bin/appcfg.sh request_logs myapp\war mylog.txt
```

Listing 9-3. *Download log files on Windows*

```
appengine-java-sdk\bin\appcfg.cmd request_logs myapp\war mylog.txt
```

Integration

Not every cloud platform can meet the needs of every enterprise challenge. However, it's common, especially in cloud-based application architectures, to integrate some of the leading cloud platforms to meet the needs of your business. This is what is sometimes called the "Cloud of Clouds," an application architecture that spans multiple cloud platforms. In this next section we're going to walk through two examples of connecting the clouds. First, we'll take a look at interacting with Google Wave, the next-generation communication and collaboration platform from Google. After that, we'll integrate with Salesforce.com, another leading platform as a service provider.

Integration with Google Wave

Google Wave is a new tool for communication and collaboration on the web. It was announced at Google I/O 2009 and is already available for early preview by over 100,000 developers. Google Wave is a hybrid e-mail /IM/document solution that is built on XMPP. Instead of communicating through e-mail threads, you use waves, which are part conversation and part document. All the users that have been added to the conversation can add content, images, video, and even maps. Each user in the conversation can see in real time what other users are typing, editing, or adding to the wave. This tool is sure to change the way we communicate electronically and drive innovation in a way that we haven't seen since instant messaging was introduced. We'll briefly touch on the types of APIs or extensions that are available with Google Wave.

Google Wave Gadgets

Google Wave allows you to embed almost any Google Gadget into a conversation. Gadgets allow non-Wave code elements or programs to interact with the users in the conversation. Gadgets exist for scenarios like multiple users collaborating on a map, users playing chess against each other, and adding photos or uploading files.

Gadgets are more interface oriented and aren't something we'll be covering in this book. Unlike, Google Wave Robots, which require App Engine, gadgets can be built on any platform. For more information on Google Wave Gadgets reference the online documentation at `http://code.google.com/apis/wave`.

Google Wave Robots

The Google Wave Robot API works a bit differently. It's a programmatic way to interact with the conversation thread without requiring a user interface. Wave Robots are automated participants in a wave and are notified via XMPP of any updates or additions to the wave. They can then respond accordingly and add contextual information to the wave or embed a gadget on the fly.

Wave Robots can talk with users and interact with the wave by adding content from outside sources. Consider the case where two friends or colleagues are discussing the stock market. Each time they mention a stock in the conversation, the robot can chime in with some useful details like current quotes, news about that stock, or historical trending. At this time, robots are only supported as Google App Engine hosted applications. The ability to build an application that can intelligently contribute to a conversation in real time is pretty appealing. You're going to create a simple robot that will send a welcome message to a group that is added to a wave and that will respond when someone mentions Apress.

■ **Note** Google Wave should be released around the time of this book's publication. If you're following these examples and Wave is still in preview mode, you can use the Account Request form at `https://services.google.com/fb/forms/wavesignupfordev` to request access to the Developer Sandbox.

Before you can create the project in Eclipse, you need to gather a few prerequisites, the first being a few .jar files that you need in order to receive and respond to requests from Wave. Navigate to `http://code.google.com/p/wave-robot-java-client/downloads/list` and download the following files:

- `jsonrpc.jar`

- `json.jar`

- `wave-robot-api-version.jar`

Next, you need to decide on an application ID for the robot. Remember, App Engine allows you to register only 10 application IDs. You can't rename or remove them once they've been created. If you'd rather reuse one from a previous example in the book, you can just change the version number and the application's default version in the Administration Console, as demonstrated earlier in this chapter. In this example, we'll use `apresswave` as the application ID, as shown in Figure 9-8.

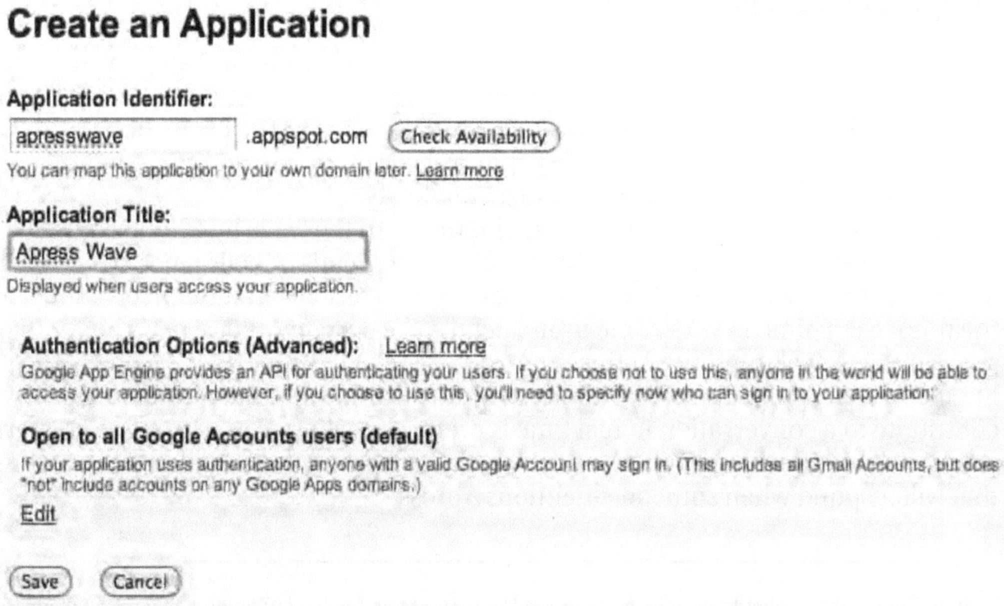

Create an Application

Application Identifier:

apresswave   .appspot.com   (Check Availability)

You can map this application to your own domain later. Learn more

Application Title:

Apress Wave

Displayed when users access your application.

Authentication Options (Advanced):   Learn more

Google App Engine provides an API for authenticating your users. If you choose not to use this, anyone in the world will be able to access your application. However, if you choose to use this, you'll need to specify now who can sign in to your application:

Open to all Google Accounts users (default)

If your application uses authentication, anyone with a valid Google Account may sign in. (This includes all Gmail Accounts, but does "not" include accounts on any Google Apps domains.)

Edit

(Save)   (Cancel)

Figure 9-8. Registering the App Engine ID for the Google Wave Robot

Now you're ready to create the Web Application Project in Eclipse. Make sure you uncheck the Google Web Toolkit for this project. Google Web Toolkit is currently only supported on Java 1.5, while Google Wave requires Java 1.6. In addition, you're not going to be building a user interface for this project, so GWT isn't needed. Set your namespace to com.kyleroche.wave so you can easily copy the sample code.

If your project defaults to Java 1.5, you will need to right-click the JRE System Library folder in the Eclipse Package Explorer and select Properties. A dialog similar to the one in Figure 9-9 will appear. Select a 1.6 JRE to ensure that you're using a supported version for the Google Wave SDK.

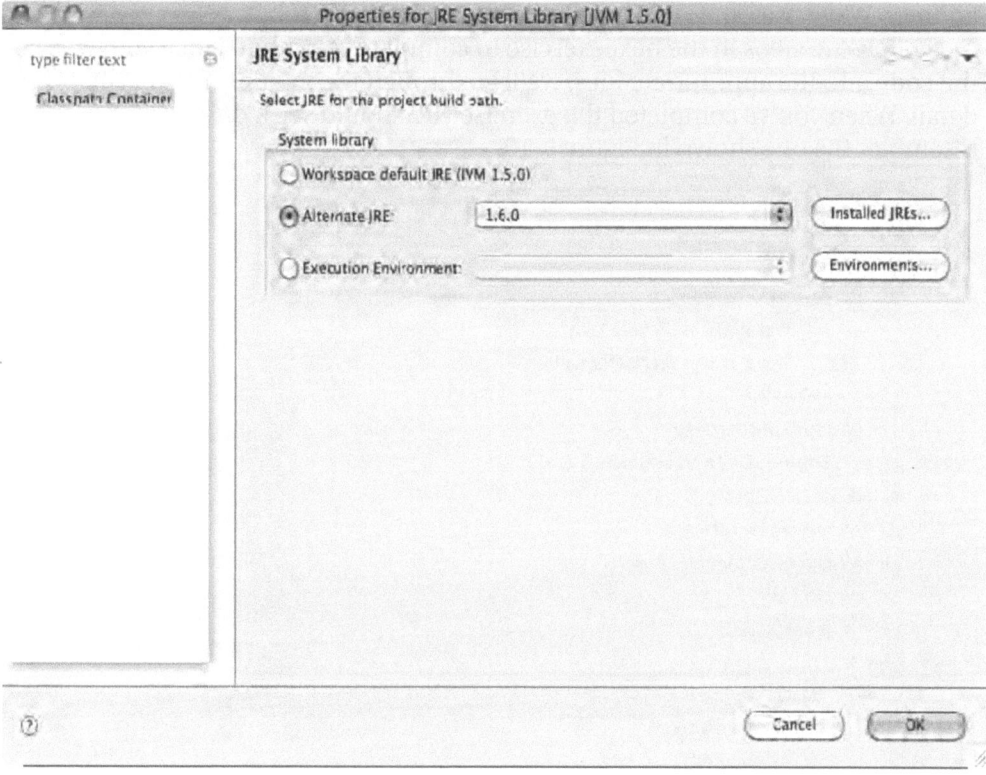

Figure 9-9. *Using an alternate JRE in an Eclipse project*

Now that you've created your project and set the appropriate JRE for Google Wave, you can copy the SDK files into the project. Drag and drop the three files you downloaded from Google Code to the war/WEB-INF/lib directory. After the three .jar files appear in the Package Explorer, right-click them and select Build Path ➤ Add to Build Path. This will create another directory in your project called Referenced Libraries with the Google Wave libraries. You're ready to add the code.

A robot actively participates in the wave through HTTP requests and responses using the Wave Robot Protocol. The files that you just added to your build path encapsulate that protocol so you can manage your robot without worrying about the underlying protocol. Currently, as mentioned, Wave only supports robots built on App Engine, which identifies applications using their application.appspot.com web address. When a user adds a robot as a participant in a wave, they use the participant address of application@appspot.com. Even though this appears to be an e-mail address, Wave uses an HTTP mechanism to contact the robot.

Follow the steps in the next exercise to complete the robot. Once you have copied the code into the appropriate files, we'll go through the major functions in more detail. When you've completed the exercise you should see a directory structure that resembles the one shown in Figure 9-10.

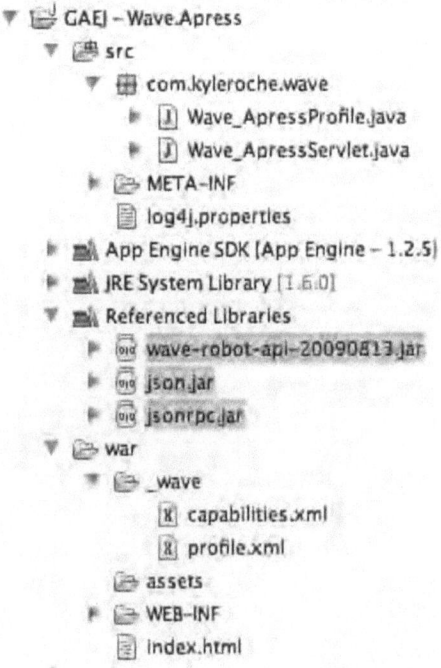

Figure 9-10. *The desired application structure*

Creating the Google Wave Robot

The following steps will complete your Google Wave Robot. You need to create a servlet to respond to the HTTP POST requests from Wave, a servlet to describe your robot to Wave, and some configuration files for Wave. After you've copied the following code to the newly created files, you'll test out the Wave Robot, and then we'll examine the code in more detail.

It's crucial that you edit your web.xml file with the contents shown in Listing 9-8. Google Wave sends HTTP POST requests to /_wave/jsonrpc each time an event occurs in a wave. Without that mapping your robot won't respond to any requests.

1. Create two servlets in the src/com.kyleroche.wave directory.

   - Wave_ApressProfile.java
   - Wave_ApressServlet.java

2. Create a subdirectory under /war called _wave. Create two files in that directory.

   - capabilities.xml
   - profile.xml

3. Copy the code from Listing 9-4 to Wave_ApressProfile.java.

4. Copy the code from Listing 9-5 to Wave_ApressServlet.java.

5. Copy the code from Listing 9-6 to capabilities.xml.

6. Copy the code from Listing 9-7 to profile.xml.

7. Copy the code from Listing 9-8 to your existing web.xml file.

8. Deploy your application to App Engine.

After you've completed these steps you'll be able to interact with your robot in a wave.

Listing 9-4. *Wave_ApressProfile.java*

```
package com.kyleroche.wave;
import com.google.wave.api.ProfileServlet;

public class Wave_ApressProfile extends ProfileServlet{

@Override
    public String getRobotName() {
            return "Apress Wave";
    }
}
```

Listing 9-5. *Wave_ApressServlet.java*

```
package com.kyleroche.wave;
import java.util.regex.Pattern;
```

```java
import com.google.wave.api.*;

public class Wave_ApressServlet extends AbstractRobotServlet{

    @Override
    public void processEvents(RobotMessageBundle bundle) {
        Wavelet wavelet = bundle.getWavelet();

        if (bundle.wasSelfAdded()){
            Blip b = wavelet.appendBlip();
            TextView t = b.getDocument();
            t.append("This is the welcome message when I join a
Wave");
        }

        for (Event e : bundle.getEvents()) {
            if (e.getType() == EventType.BLIP_SUBMITTED) {
                submit(wavelet, e.getBlip());
            }
        }
    }

    private void submit(Wavelet wavelet, Blip blip)
    {
        TextView t = blip.getDocument();
        String str = t.getText();
        if (Pattern.matches("apress", str)) {
            t.append("\n\nHow's the book?");
        }
    }
}
```

Listing 9-6. *capabilities.xml*

```xml
<?xml version="1.0" encoding="utf-8"?>
<w:robot xmlns:w="http://wave.google.com/extensions/robots/1.0">
  <w:capabilities>
    <w:capability name="BLIP_SUBMITTED" content="true" />
  </w:capabilities>
  <w:version>0.6</w:version>
  <w:profile name="Wave_Apress" profileurl="/_wave/profile.xml"/>
</w:robot>
```

Listing 9-7. profile.xml

```xml
<?xml version="1.0"?>
<wagent-profile>Wave_Apress</wagent-profile>
```

Listing 9-8. web.xml

```xml
<servlet>
    <servlet-name>Wave_ApressServlet</servlet-name>
    <servlet-class>com.kyleroche.wave.Wave_ApressServlet</servlet-class>
</servlet>
<servlet>
<servlet-name>Profile</servlet-name>
            <servlet-
class>com.kyleroche.wave.Wave_ApressProfile</servlet-class>
 </servlet>

  <servlet-mapping>
    <servlet-name>Profile</servlet-name>
    <url-pattern>/_wave/robot/profile</url-pattern>
  </servlet-mapping>

<servlet-mapping>
<servlet-name>Wave_ApressServlet</servlet-name>
    <url-pattern>/_wave/robot/jsonrpc</url-pattern>
</servlet-mapping>
```

Try things out with Wave and see how your robot responds. Start a new wave. Click the New Wave button at the top of your Inbox. Click the plus sign (+) next to your profile picture at the top of your new wave. Add application@appspot.com to the wave, where "application" is the application ID of your Google App Engine project. Once the robot has been added to the conversation it will respond with the welcome message from Wave_ApressServlet.java. This response comes after you check the .wasSelfAdded() method of the event bundle that you were sent from Wave. Google Wave will send your application a bundle of "events" every time something has happened in the wave. Among dozens of other actions, events include adding participants, changing text, adding images or elements to the wave, and removing participants.

Now when the robot finds the text string "Apress" in the conversation, it will respond with "How's the book?" This is a simple example, but keep in mind that you could have easily called out to another system, enriching the conversation with relevant data from your financial system, or your CRM database. See Figure 9-11, which demonstrates both responses from your robot.

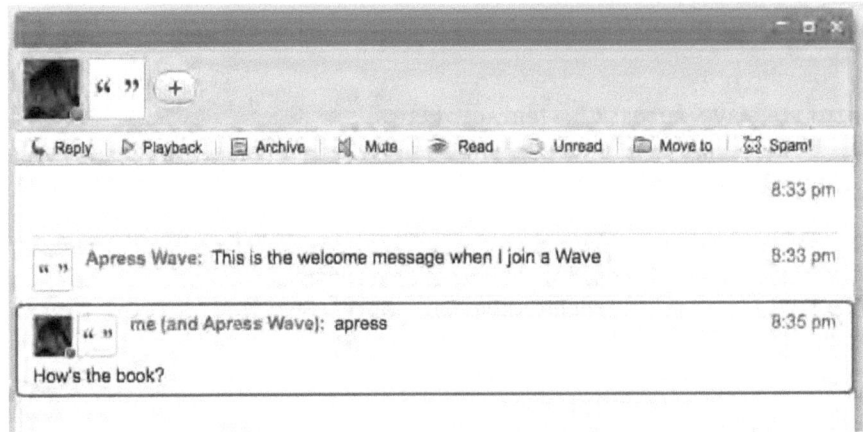

Figure 9-11. Interacting with your Google Wave Robot

Integration with Salesforce.com

Salesforce.com is used by millions of people for sales-force automation, CRM, case management, and much more. In addition to the Software as a Service offerings like Salesforce.com CRM, Salesforce.com's Force.com platform powers high-traffic community sites like http://mystarbucksidea.force.com/, http://www.ideastorm.com, and http://pledge5.starbucks.com. Force.com and Google Apps have been collaborating on numerous solutions since the launch of Google Apps to bring the two cloud offerings together.

Before App Engine was released, Google and Salesforce.com had 10 integration options that were shipping with every Salesforce.com org. In Salesforce.com vernacular, an "org" is the equivalent of an "environment," or, more generally speaking, the segregated section of a customer's data in the multitenant environment. Recall from our earlier discussions that multitenant environments allow multiple customers to share the same data and application tiers while maintaining segregation of the actual customer data.

From attaching documents to synchronizing your contact lists, combining Google Apps, App Engine, and Salesforce.com made it possible to build more complex application architectures that met more business requirements without reverting to on-premise software. If you're building a business application for a company that uses one of Salesforce.com's offerings, you can quickly integrate the two platforms using the Force.com toolkit for Google App Engine. In the following section you'll create a Salesforce.com development org and integrate it with App Engine.

Setting Up a Salesforce.com Development Org

This isn't a Salesforce.com book, so you're not going to do anything beyond creating an org and pulling data from the org to your App Engine application. To create your Free Developer Edition org, browse to http://developer.force.com and locate the Get a Free Developer Edition link. Follow the instructions and fill in the form to receive your developer login information. You'll receive an e-mail with an activation link. Follow that link to set your password, and you'll be automatically logged in to your new Development Edition org.

To minimize the amount of discussion on Force.com and to remain focused on App Engine, we're going to take a few security shortcuts in this example. Force.com uses a Security Token for each user to authenticate via the API. To avoid having to deal with Security Tokens, you're going to open your Development Edition org so that you can receive requests from any IP address without a Security Token. This is not a recommended practice for a production environment.

Click the Setup link at the top-right corner of your Salesforce.com org. Use the navigation tree in the left panel to open the Security Controls ➤ Network Access utility, as shown in Figure 9-12. Click New and add 75.101.133.136 as the start and end IP address of the entry.

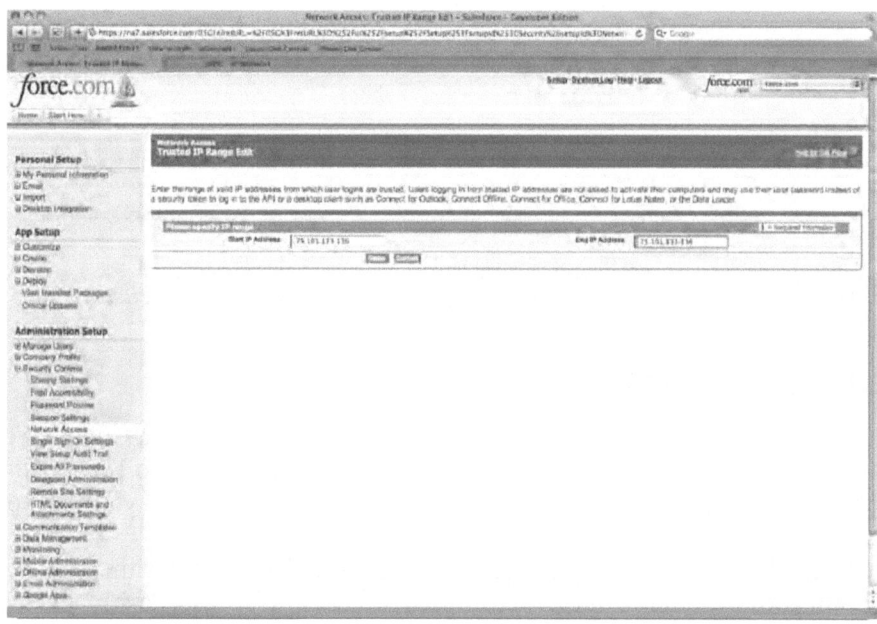

Figure 9-12. *Network Access configuration in Salesforce.com*

You're going to use a publicly available service for whitelisting (adding all IP addresses to your Trusted IP Range) your org. Navigate to `http://appirio.net/whitelist` in your browser. Enter your Salesforce.com credentials, as shown in Figure 9-13, and click the Go button. That's all the Salesforce.com work you'll be doing in this book. You can close that window if you want.

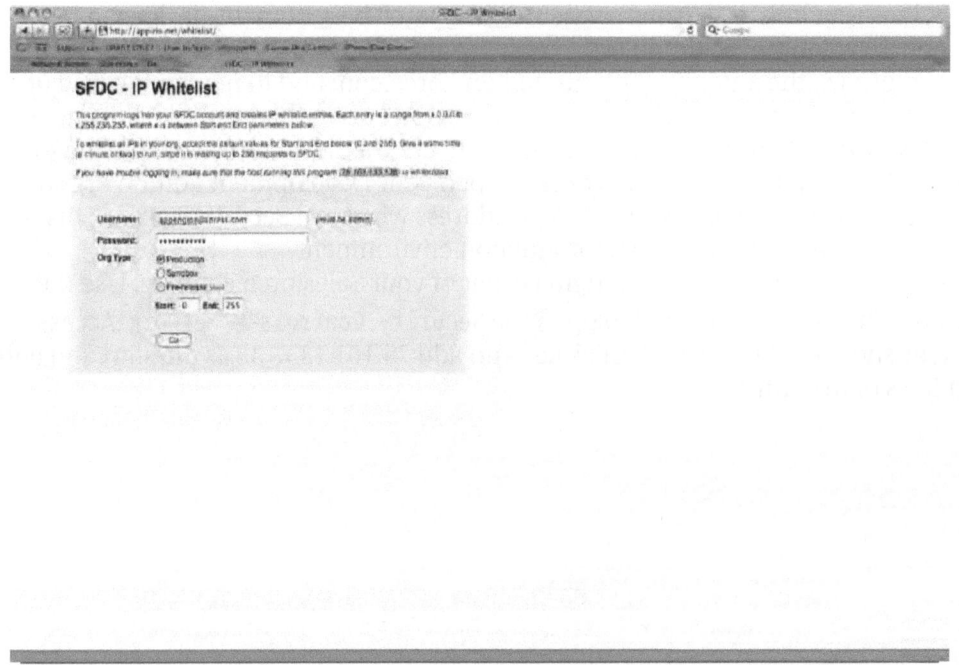

Figure 9-13. *Whitelisting your Salesforce.com org using the Appirio IP Whitelisting tool*

Connecting to the Development Org

Create a new Web Application Project in Eclipse. Make sure you uncheck Google Web Toolkit. As with the Google Wave example, you need to change the JRE to 1.6 to use the Saleforce.com libraries. Reference Figure 9-9 earlier in this chapter if you skipped the Google Wave example.

As with Google Wave, you need to download the libraries to interact with Force.com. Point your browser to `http://code.google.com/p/sfdc-wsc/downloads/list` and download the `partner-library.jar` file and the `wsc-gae-version.jar`. Similar to the steps in the preceding example, you need to add these files to the `war/WEB-INF/lib`

directory of your project. Right-click the project directory in Eclipse and select Build
Path ➤ Add to Build Path. Open the servlet that was automatically created for you
under your src folder. Ours was called HelloWorldServlet.java. Copy the code from
Listing 9-9 into the servlet.

Listing 9-9. Code for the servlet

```java
package com.kyleroche.sfdcwsc;

import java.io.IOException;
import java.io.PrintWriter;
import javax.servlet.http.*;
import com.sforce.ws.*;
import com.sforce.soap.partner.*;
import com.sforce.soap.partner.sobject.SObject;

@SuppressWarnings("serial") public class HelloWorldServlet extends
HttpServlet {
        private String username = "appengine@apress.com";
        private String password = "app1r10#123";
        private PartnerConnection connection;

        public void doGet(HttpServletRequest req, HttpServletResponse resp)
throws IOException {                                resp.setContentType("text/html");

                resp.getWriter().println("Hello, from Salesforce.com");
                                PrintWriter t = resp.getWriter();
                getConnection( t, req);
                if ( connection == null ) { return; }
                QueryResult result = null;

                try {
                        result = connection.query("select name from Account
                limit 10");
                } catch (ConnectionException e) {
                        e.printStackTrace();
                }

                for (SObject account : result.getRecords()) {
                        t.println("<li>"+ (String)account.getField("Name") +
                "</li>");
                }
        }
```

```
void getConnection(PrintWriter out, HttpServletRequest req)  {

    ConnectorConfig config = new ConnectorConfig();

    config.setUsername(username);
    config.setPassword(password);
    connection = Connector.newConnection(config);
  }
}
```

Once you've completed the code, deploy your application. Browse to the application in your browser. You should see the default `index.html` file that was created with the Web Application Project template. Click the listing for the servlet where you added the code from Listing 9-9. You should see something similar to Figure 9-14. Salesforce.com creates a default set of accounts in Development orgs, so you should have the same record set.

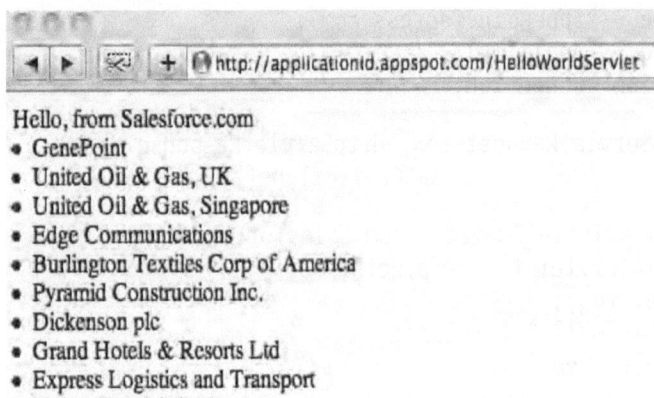

Listing 9-14. Salesforce.com integration from Google App Engine

Summary

In this chapter we introduced you to application administration and integration with other services like Salesforce.com and Google Wave to demonstrate how easy it is to connect App Engine applications to leading cloud platforms. Starting off with the App Engine Administration Console, you viewed your list of application IDs and learned how to version applications. You used the dashboard to analyze usage statistics, and you used the App Engine Log utility to do some basic application troubleshooting.

After briefly looking at the administration options available to App Engine administrators, you constructed two examples of integrations with Google App Engine. First, you used App Engine to create a robot for Google Wave. After having a conversation with your robot in a wave, you integrated with Salesforce.com.

We had a great time writing this book. It was exciting to work with Google App Engine so soon after its release. We wanted to show you a number of features rather than dive too deeply into any one area. We hope we've armed you with a broad understanding of the possibilities of Google App Engine, and we look forward to seeing your innovative applications come to life very soon.

Index

You Need the Companion eBook